MW01611152

LORD, DON'T MIND THE MULE, JUST LOAD THE WAGON

Doyle Moody

Permission to reprint: It would be my pleasure to have my stories quoted. I also give permission to those who would like to reprint a paragraph or two if appropriate credit is given. The following credit should be used: "From Lord, Don't Mind the Mule, Just Load the Wagon, by Doyle Moody."

The Bible quotations throughout the text were quoted from the New International Version of the Bible, published in 1988 by Biblia.

I would also like to gratefully acknowledge quoting from or paraphrasing text from the following: Dietrich Bonhoeffer's The Cost of Discipleship, Dr. David Jeremiah's A Bend in the Road, John Francis Tenney's Slavery, Secession, and Success, and Margery Williams' The Velveteen Rabbit.

Lord, Don't Mind the Mule,
Just Load the Wagon

Published 2011 by Old Kings Road Press
Flagler Beach, Florida

ISBN 10: 1-60179-056-2
ISBN 13: 978-1-60179-056-9

To order additional copies contact Doyle Moody
31 Beachside Drive
Palm Coast, Florida 32137

dontmindthemule@gmail.com

ACKNOWLEDGEMENTS

There are several individuals I want to thank for helping me get this project done:

Marianne Lumbard, for her insistence on my finishing after laying this writing aside for years.

Marianne, my wife, and Anna Marie, my daughter, for their encouragement and help with editing. I cannot tell you how many times Marianne has patiently read through the text. Anna Marie also took the picture of the mule and the wagon for the cover.

Charles and Susan Medcalf, for providing the mule in the photo on the cover.

Ann Stewart, my sister, for typing my first copy. I wrote the whole text in longhand.

Jan Elliott, my very first critic on a very rough copy, which she followed up with a beautiful letter.

Janis Bosworth, my neighbor, for helping type some chapters in the beginning, and again, for helping with editing in the end.

The Ticknor family, for the uplifting Christian encouragement I needed; Shirley, the mom, who explained why I didn't start writing as a young man. She said, "Doyle, you didn't have any stories then."

Bishop Frank and Emmy Cerveny – Emmy has been one of my best cheerleaders (without these, some of us have problems finishing the game); and Frank, for his kind words in the foreword of this book and his words of wisdom for my spiritual life.

Through the years after starting this venture, I knew all along there would have to be someone with typing skills and editing ability to help me. I might say here that this would not be just an ordinary person. I don't type at all, I write very poorly, and I spell worse. But the Lord knew all this, too. He sent to our church Herb and Beverley Hasenbalg – two fine Christians. When Beverley heard of my wanting to finish my book, she offered to help, not really knowing what she was getting herself into.

I cannot describe on this page what a blessing Beverley has been to me on this endeavor – not just her skills, but her encouragement to a first-time writer. I pray that God will bless her for using her patience and talents on my book. Without her, it would never have become a reality. I love you, Beverley.

Doyle Moody

DEDICATION

I would like to dedicate this book to my wife, Marianne, because of her love and continued support in standing beside me through the ups and downs of 57 years of marriage. When I failed, she encouraged me to get up and try again; when I succeeded, she bragged on me. Her never-failing love of our Lord and her desire to worship Him every Sunday are an inspiration to me.

Marianne took care of my mom during almost all of our married life. This started when my dad died after we had been married only several years. Marianne continued to take care of her most of these years in our home – through a fractured back. She then nursed her back to health with over 100 physical exercises every morning. She continued caring for her during the decline of Mom's mind and having to bathe her until her 100th birthday. We finally had to put Mom in an assisted living home, and she died about two months shy of 104 in 2010. I do not know of another wife that would do this for her mother-in-law. I will never be able to thank her enough, but I feel that God will take care of it someday, and bless her for her job here on earth.

I also thank her for the encouragement she gave me while I was writing this book. There are no words to tell you how she kept me going. May God richly bless her in this life and the one to come.

I love you, Marianne.
Doyle
August 9, 2011

SPECIAL THANKS

I would like to offer a very special thanks to my four children for all their hard work when growing up. I had the desire to work for myself and be my own boss, and they all worked very hard and gave up a lot of their childhood for this. We all worked so hard, and it never happened. I pray that God will bless each of them for their labor. Also, I would like to thank each of them for the love they show me now and for not holding their childhood labor against me.

Ben, Gary, Anna Marie, and Keith,
I love you,
Dad
August 9, 2011

FOREWORD

Life is a journey, and Doyle Moody has lived his well. His purpose in writing his book is to share stories of his life experiences with his children and grandchildren. What he has produced is a deeply profound look into a life lived with humility and a deep faith in God.

Doyle writes with freedom and clarity of life in the rural South when the simpler pleasures were what gave life meaning. He even rejoices in the midst of hardships, reflecting that "Adversity is a place to rest your head while climbing higher."

Doyle Moody has climbed life's mountains and is wise to the world's challenges, strong in his belief that the Lord is his rock and salvation. I wholeheartedly recommend this book written by a man who is pure in heart and guided by the Spirit of God.

Frank S. Cerveny, IV
Bishop of the Episcopal Diocese of Florida

INTRODUCTION
DECEMBER 1995

I must make a start.

What is this book about and why did I write it? I want my family to know me better - the family now in 1996 and the ones that will follow. What was I like and what did I think about? What was life like in these times? My mom, dad and grandparents told me lots of stories about life in their times, and nothing was ever written down. So these little bits and pieces of life will come to an end if I don't make this attempt.

Another thing that helped me get interested in writing was a little book my wife's great-grandfather wrote about coming to Florida in 1859. It was called Slavery, Secession and Success (Tenney, John Francis, Southern Literary Institute, San Antonio, Texas 1934, pp 7-8). After reading this about just what was going on in his life and what times were like, I was encouraged to try to do the same. I remember every sentence in the short book was so valuable to me. Here are a few words in his first chapter: "After we had crossed the bar at the mouth of the St. Johns River a fellow-passenger, pointing to the shores informed me that I had 'seen all Florida,' meaning the whole State was flat and uninteresting, like what I saw.

"In due time we reached what they called 'The City of Jacksonville," but what was simply a little village – and a poor one at that. There was one good hotel – the Judson House – run by O.L. Keene; two saw mills, two good stores – one was built of brick, the only brick building in the city, and run by C.L. Robinson; a few scattered dwelling houses here and there; a post-office; bar room; but had not arrived to the dignity of sidewalks or paved streets."

Have you ever thought about what you are going to leave when you are gone? I get to thinking about this sometimes. Someone dies, you go to the funeral, wish the family well, and say, "I'll be praying for you." The person that is gone will be talked about a few days or weeks and then a memory now and then, and soon they are in the past. What will I leave? I don't have a million dollars, but suppose I did. There are homes in the area worth that and more. Or maybe the home would be passed down to the children. You might know I'm a deer hunter, and as I walk in the woods and come up on some old bricks and I say, "Looks like there was an old home here once." So the brick home won't stay either. That's all that is left. It will go, too. Who was here and what was it like back then? I have reached the age that causes me to wonder what it was like back then, and maybe you are getting there, too.

So I believe the manmade material things we leave and the money will be gone in years to come as we see of others in the past. I believe words can be passed on and not lose so much of their value as cars, houses, money, and "things," as I call it. Words, if not changed, don't go bad, rot, spoil, shrink, expand or lose their value as much. I think they can be of great value and interest for years to come.

I've never heard about someone having Moses' staff, or nails from Christ's cross, bones off the big fish that swallowed Jonah, a sample of preserved manna or some wine from the wedding feast that Jesus helped them out with when the wine was running short. On the other hand, when Jesus said this is how we should pray – "Our Father who art in Heaven" – surely a lot of generations still know these words. Not in stone or cast in metal, but someone wrote them down and passed them on. David said to someone – "The Lord is my shepherd," God even gave Moses the Ten Commandments in stone and they got destroyed, but we managed to pass them on. We have many famous sayings from presidents, governors, poets, dads, moms and grandparents.

So I believe words are one of the most valuable things we can leave.

I recently heard a speaker preparing the area for the Billy Graham crusade coming to Jacksonville, Florida, in November 2000. He said, "Don't forget, what's down in the well comes up in the bucket." So maybe these words and thoughts are in my "well" and this book is my bucket. Oh, yes, I know this book will rot or burn and can be destroyed, but it could be reprinted or even better, the stories retold just the way I got them to start with. I can't remember ever reading many of them in a book.

You know many people who collect a large variety of things. Almost everything we see and use, there is a person collecting them as a hobby or maybe for profit. I'll try to name a few: old and out-of-date books, old records of music from the past, dolls, old cars, coins, stamps, things that belonged to famous people. My wife has two: one is flowers of all kinds, and the other is cookbooks – she loves to read recipes. What is yours? Do you collect something?

Well, mine are not hanging on a wall, or in a filing cabinet, or in a garage, or a showcase; they are the stories I have collected in my lifetime, stored in my head, and some of them written down on these pages to be passed on to you and your families. I hope you will enjoy them, and I also hope there will be some that will be a benefit to you in some way. I have enjoyed saving them and I hope you enjoy reading them.

Lord, don't mind the mule, just load the wagon.

ABOUT THE TITLE
"LORD, DON'T MIND THE MULE, JUST LOAD THE WAGON."

I guess you can tell right off this phrase is not very modern. It's probably southern, too, but I don't know that for sure. I do know it is old. How far back, you might ask? Well, there is another old saying that might help set the time. "A long time ago when my daddy was a little boy." If I was choosing an era, this would help narrow it down.

Here in the South, back then, farming and livestock raising were a way of life. It was the way most people survived. Most folks grew and raised what they ate. They sold off a little of the extra to buy what they couldn't provide for themselves, things like cloth, shoes, flour, coffee, black pepper, salt, sugar, and the like.

To get the products from the field to the barn, from the farm to town, from town to the railroad station, most of the time it was the mule and the wagon. He was cheap and affordable transportation. He ate what you raised, very seldom broke down, was very dependable and low maintenance. He looked about the same as the neighbor's down the road, and you didn't have the problem with trading it in every couple of years for a fancier model with more options like C.D. players, AC, four-wheel drive, chrome wheels, leather seats, and a candy apple red paint job. No, all mules were about the same, new or old; they ate whatever you put in the manger and whatever grass they could pick up during the day. On a cold winter morning you just patted your mule on the side of the neck and said, "Come on, Emma, let's go," and she was ready; no dead battery, empty tank, or flat tires to worry with.

With living conditions much tougher than they are today, every trip with a mule and wagon had to count. No big John Deere tractor and rubber-tired carts in the field, no refrigerated semis over the road, and no big jumbo jets to carry the products to their markets. To the farmer telling his wife, his children, or his neighbor, "Don't mind the mule, just load the wagon," was a way of saying, "We've got to make every load count; pile it high, my mule can handle it." Every farmer had pride in what his mule could do.

The mule is a hybrid animal and is a cross between a female horse and a male donkey. I suppose they were chosen for their powerful ability to pull heavy loads and work for long periods of time in the fields with little care. The mule is a very powerful animal, but, at times, seems to be very stubborn. So that old saying, "stubborn as a mule," meant more than a stubborn old animal. I read up on mules, and it said the mule is more intelligent than the horse. The stubbornness seems to come from being very cautious. They are slower and more sure footed than the horse so as not to get hurt in whatever situation you put them in. I saw that the army has started using them again to carry supplies in dangerous areas.

Crossing two species can produce a third, often better and more suitable to certain conditions. You treat them right, they treat you right. Very simple. Like humans, they inherit certain characteristics from both sides. From the father (donkey), the mule gets intelligence, long ears, and small hooves for surefootedness. From the mother (horse), they get cooperative disposition, endurance, strength, and, of course, size. The mule seems to have the sobriety, patience, and surefootedness of the donkey, and the vigor and courage of the horse. People have generally found that mules show less impatience under pressure of heavy loads and their skin is harder and less sensitive to sun and rain. Their hooves are harder, and the mule also shows a natural resistance to disease and insects. They seem to be less tolerant of dogs and capable of striking with any hoof in any direction. Well, so much as to why I chose the mule.

Coming out of a doctor's office one day, I read a plaque on the wall that said, "Adversity doesn't build character, it reveals it."

We all have had or are going to have adversity in our lives. These stumbling blocks can help us become stronger or can break us down. We must choose. If it is as the plaque said, and reveals character as to what's on the inside, then we need to work on this in every attempt the devil makes on us. What have we ever learned to help us and our family and friends when times were good and things were great? Not much, I'm afraid. The tough times are where we really learn about true life.

I'll never forget one of my morning readings years ago about the little boy and his sister climbing the steep hill. One was complaining about all the rocks in their path up the hill. The other said, "Where else would you put your feet?" Adversity, is it a place to put your foot while climbing higher or is it just more rocks in your path?

I have chosen this old saying because I want to claim this in my life. Lord, don't mind the mule, just load the wagon. Yes, I wish I could get up each morning and say, "Lord, whatever you have for me today, bring it on. With your help, I can handle it." If the load be light or heavy, mine or someone else's, I would know I could, like the old mule, handle it. I'm not there yet, but I'm working on it.

One more mention of the mule. My very close friend and brother in Christ, Tommy Purvis, gave a meditation on a weekend retreat many years ago. It was about helping his dad in the swamp when he was a small boy. His dad was in the logging business, and Tommy was helping as much as he could at his age. Tommy was always afraid of getting lost in the woods and separated from his dad. If the sawmill was down and he couldn't hear it running, he wouldn't know which direction his home was. So his dad always assured him he could just get on the old mule, let the mule do the leading, and he would take him to the barn. The mule knew where he was being fed was his home. (That's a whole lesson in itself.) This was one of the very best meditations I was blessed to hear. I can still picture in my mind Tommy as a small boy trusting in that old mule to take him to the open woods so he could get home. As we see each other several times a year, we still talk about the trip on the mule's back.

I believe Paul, in his letters, might have achieved this closer than anyone I have ever read about.

In II Corinthians 6:4 he says: "Rather as servants

of God we commend ourselves in every way, in great endurance; in troubles, hardships and distress in beatings, imprisonments and riots; in hard work, sleepless nights and hunger; in purity, understanding, patience, and kindness in the Holy Spirit and in sincere love."

On top of all these things and being put in chains and in prison for preaching the Gospel, Paul had something else he called a thorn in the flesh. We all have one, don't we? He asked the Lord three times to take it away, and God said, "My grace is sufficient for you, for my power is made perfect in weakness," (II Corinthians 12:9).

So, Paul says, "That is why, for Christ's sake, I delight in weakness, in insults, in hardships, in persecutions, in difficulties, for when I am weak, then I am strong," (II Corinthians 12:10).

If someday I could learn to use life's adversity to make my life better, my faith stronger, and help enrich the lives of people I meet, then and only then can I say, and really mean it, "Lord, don't mind the mule, just load the wagon."

CHAPTER 1
RETIREMENT

In February of 1999, I retired. Never thought I would be able to, but God has blessed me to see the day where we don't have to set that alarm clock to meet someone's beckoning call. It could mean you just can't wait to get started on that boat you've been wanting to build, or to play golf in the middle of the week when it is less crowded. Or, it could be that you'll bring that old sewing machine out and make that dress you've been putting off for years. Or maybe I'll get started on the book I've been wanting to read. But, I've been so worn out from working that about one page is all I could read at a time. I guess one of the nicest things is the choice we have. If we decide to start tomorrow instead of today, we can do that. At work, we don't usually have that choice. When I get through mowing the grass, I can come in and cool off or even better yet, after lunch I can take a nap. One job I had in the paper mill was running some tests on the chemicals and wood pulp we were bleaching. I ran the same test every hour for about twelve years. You know that can become very boring. I'm sure not bored anymore.

My retirement started out a little slow. I had to start some of my prostate cancer treatment just before retirement, so that when I retired the doctors could finish their work. This left me sort of limited as to what I was able to do. I remember my first fishing trip to the beach after cancer treatment. I didn't know if I was going to get back to the house or not. Of course, eventually I did get back on my feet with the fine care of my wife. Marianne was a good nurse, and I was so thankful for her. As soon as I got over the worst of the side effects and on my feet, my wife, Marianne, had a hysterectomy. I was glad I was home and able to help her. She looked after me for so long, it was a good feeling to repay a little of it. After her being active for so long as a mail carrier in St. Augustine, it was hard to picture me having to help her out of bed for the slow trip to the bathroom. Needless to say, we both had been in the house for a while on our retirement venture.

Then one beautiful spring morning, I just needed to see the sky. Ever been there? Cooking – which I knew little about – washing clothes, and all that, goes with housework. I just needed to step outside for a second. By now she could get up by herself pretty well.

I just opened the front door and stepped outside to take a breath and say to myself, "Boy, this is great." I didn't even close the door. My friend, Gray Craven, had called the day before to check on us and see how we were doing. He wanted to lift my spirits with a "shore nuff" fish tale. Seems he and his son took their boat just outside Matanzas Inlet to fish for whiting – small fish, small tackle, and light lines. Well, what do they get into but a school of big red bass, my favorite fish to catch. I'm talking about 35 and 40 pounders. Well, lines were broken and fish were released (they were all over the legal limit), but it turned out to be a fun day. Now, it's only about four blocks from our home to the beach, and I could just picture the surf being full of those reds. I thought, no, I'm not going, Marianne needs me at home. I hung up the phone and told her the story, and of course she said I should go right then, she would be OK. I said no, but, if I had a fresh mullet for bait, I would dash over there. Taking time to go catch a fresh mullet was out of the question for me.

So as I was standing there getting a little fresh air, I heard this loud racket overhead, and here comes a big bald eagle and an osprey fighting over a fish. I still don't know which one had it, but it was clear the battle was on. In the heat of the fight, the one that had the fish dropped it! Where do you think they dropped it? Yes, right in my front yard about 20 feet from where I was standing. What kind of fish? Right again, a nice fresh mullet about 12 inches long and still alive. (You can't beat that for fresh.)

Marianne had gotten out of bed and had walked to the front door, not seeing the commotion going on overhead. All she saw was me picking something up from the yard.

As I picked up the mullet by the tail and him still wiggling, she said, “What in the world have you got?” Well, with a big grin, I called back, “Guess I’ve got that fresh mullet I wanted, and I might have to run over to the beach, after all.”

So, I did grab my old surf rod and ran over for a short fishing trip and to relax. It was fun, and then I was thinking, if I caught a big old red bass, who in the world would believe this story? Well, I didn’t catch a fish, but it was a great way to start retirement, and maybe the bait story is enough.

I can still see that big bald eagle flying up in a pine tree across the road from where he (or the osprey) dropped the mullet and watching me take his dinner to my house. If he could talk, I’m sure his story wouldn’t be as exciting as mine.

While we’re on the subject of blessings falling out of the sky, what about the 16th chapter of Exodus? The Israelites were putting the bad mouth on Moses and Aaron because food was so scarce, and the Lord said to Moses, “I will rain down bread from Heaven for you.” Right in their camp (or yard). They didn’t have to grow it, kill it, wash it, cook it, buy it or store it, ‘cause there would be more for them tomorrow. What more could you ask for when the groceries run short? God is good.

So, if you can believe this story we have used for quite some time now, you ought not to have any trouble believing He can arrange for that eagle to drop off a mullet for old Doyle to fish with (a live one, at that).

What am I doing in retirement? Why, I’ve got an old Jeep to rebuild, a nice yard to keep up, an old rocker to repaint, an old school desk to refinish, a book to finish writing, and, most of all, a good God to praise and worship every day.

Lord, don’t mind the mule, just load the wagon.

CHAPTER 2
AS A CHILD

Somewhere in my late 40's I began to think about writing about some things in life that seemed so different as to the daily norm. It seemed the older I got, the more comparisons I was making. The way of life, people, prices, change in general, and then the change in me. Well, maybe I need to write some of this down so my children and grandchildren know what I was like, and tell them about some of the times we lived in, but what about my grandchildren? Will they want to know what Pa Pa was like and what life was like in his time?

I get to thinking about how birthday parties are now, for the little ones. Only last week a friend told me about his grandson's birthday party. They had rented some place where the kids would have room to play and all the video games they wanted to play for $150.00, and of course, hamburgers and drinks after. I thought back to a time when I was small and Mama told me I could have whatever I wanted for my birthday. Didn't even have to ponder on it - I wanted watermelon and fried bologna. See what I mean? Times have changed.

My grandchildren are watching cartoons on TV every Saturday morning. That's just what you do. My grandpa was telling me stories about Brer Rabbit and the fox in the 1930's and early 40's and for the life of me I have no idea where he got them from. It was surely some special entertainment.

Of course, like everyone else, I joined in with the modern times and took my nine cents and went to the picture show (movie) every Saturday to see my heroes, Roy Rogers and Gene Autry. What cowboys they were!

The rest of the week I could walk out my back door to my own corral. There were two sticks drove in the ground about four feet apart and three feet high with a stick nailed across on top to make my hitching post. I cut a piece of bamboo about six feet long from the corner of our yard, split it a few inches on the big end to put a string in it for my bridle. I can't tell you how many miles I rode that old horse, then tied him up to the rail till tomorrow. What good clean fun it was.

Of course, every cowboy had to have a cow whip. I got to see the cowboys in the picture show, and also at my dad's cousin's who had cattle, hogs, and horses and was raised on the land in Clay County where my grandpa grew up. We went out to his place a lot when I was little. Everyone knew who Sweet Moody was. His name was Benjamin, but I never heard anyone call him anything but Sweet. If he was around and on his horse when we drove up, he would always take the long cow whip off the saddle, swing it around once or twice, and pull it back for a pop that sounded like a rifle shot.

Grandpa saw how much I liked it. One day when we got around some cypress logs that were fresh cut and on the ground, Grandpa stripped off some long strips of the bark. Seems like they were strips about a half inch or so wide and six or seven feet long. Then he used about three or four strips and plaited them together. With some cotton string, he tied this to a round wooden handle about a foot long. Then on the end of the whip, he tied a number of cotton strings together to form the cracker on the end. That's what makes the noise and where we get our name from – "Florida Cracker." The noise is like the one that you made when you got after your brother or sister with the dish towel and tried to give them a pop.

Anyway, I got my cow whip and was so proud of it. Grandpa was good to me and showed me many things like this when I was little. He helped me build my first bird trap. Red birds seem to love the corn the best. I always wanted me a quail to eat but never caught one. Then he could make a flute or some kind of musical instrument that would make a low-pitched sound with about three holes in it to change notes. This was made out of a squash stem that was about 16 inches long and hollow. I still can't remember how he made it. I just wish I could say I taught my grandchildren things like that, but I'm afraid I didn't do such a good job.

I always had lots of questions for him. I remember at Christmas when I was hanging my socks up for Santa Claus and wanted to know if he ever did that. He said, "Oh, yes, we hung our stockings up, too, and we would get several soda crackers (saltine crackers) and maybe an apple and a piece of chewing tobacco." Then he explained that most all little children chewed a little. They would take a leaf of cured tobacco, lay it out flat, and sprinkle a little brown sugar on it, put another leaf, and do the same until they had it as thick as they wanted. They would cut this into plugs or pieces the size they wanted, and it was ready to press.

In those days, most all the old homes in the south were sitting on huge blocks of heart yellow pine. It was very strong, it didn't rot very easily, and the termites didn't bother it much. You had to have a very stout pole to pry up the corner of the house sitting on its block, slide the tobacco plugs in, and let the house press your tobacco leaves and sugar to make your chewing tobacco. What a difference from the things in children's Christmas stockings of today.

Grandpa left me with many stories of my childhood, but one short saying I held onto to this day. He said, "You can't help who you are kin to, but you can sure help who you associate with." I've held onto that one. As I will mention in here, Grandpa traveled around a lot in Florida and south Georgia preaching. He was well known and well liked. The only pay was the collection taken at the service and divided among the preachers there that day - usually a few dollars for each. After one such service, an old lady came to him and laid in his hand a piece of paper with some coins rolled in it and twisted together on each end. He thanked her and after she walked off he unrolled the coins in the crumpled paper. There were 13 pennies rolled in the paper. He found her in the crowd and thanked her again, but he wanted to give it back, saying he was sure she needed it more than he did. She said, "Mr. Moody, that's all the money I had and I wanted you to have it." He then took her 13 cents and realized he needed to accept it as a true gift. He also said he never refused any gift after that, realizing peoples' need to give. That, he said, was the biggest gift he ever received.

So, what I am saying is, the reason for writing these stories is to tell my grandchildren what their Pa Pa was like and what times were like when I was young and what they are like today.

Have you got time for one more short one?

Another fun time I had when I was very small was with my old blue tricycle. We lived at 412 Madison Street in Palatka, Florida, so I had a good sidewalk to ride on. It went all the way around the block without crossing the street. If you have never tried this, you just missed out on a big part of growing up.

I would get a tin can out of Mama's kitchen (used, of course), like Pet milk or pork and beans size, cut the top out completely, and with the ice pick punch a small little hole in the bottom. This is where the real precise work comes in. The hole has to be just the right size so when you fill the can with water it will drip out very slowly. Then I put the can on the back step of the tricycle, tied a string around it, and used a string to tie the can to the step, which was not so easy. Now I had a gas tank.

I'd fill up my can with water at the house and start on my trip (around the block) and see if I could make it back before my gas tank was empty. I can even remember looking back at the water in the can part way around to see how I was doing. Just good clean fun, you know.

I can't help to be amazed at how toys have changed. The toy trucks with batteries and motors in them that will do almost anything that your big one will do, it's only smaller. Then I think back to my small block of wood someone had sawed out to sort of look like a truck, and had four Coca Cola caps nailed on it for the tires. Of course, they didn't roll, but it didn't seem to matter either. Just good fun down in the dirt making some tracks.

The dolls now, for little girls, are so real. They talk, wet their diaper, open and close their eyes, seem so alive. In contrast, Rosa Lee, a lady I worked with at St. Joe's in

St. Augustine, said when she was little they would pull up a clump of a certain kind of grass that had fine roots on it, turn it upside down and wash the roots, and plait them for the hair, and that was their doll.

My wife tells me the story of leaving her only doll in a neighbor's yard late one afternoon and she saw the next day that it had been burned in a trash pile. This was a yard her mom told her not to go in. A very cruel act for a small child to endure. Marianne got a small piece of round rough wood and wrapped it in a cloth for a blanket, and this was her doll for a long time, until next Christmas. She gave it the same loving care because it was her very own.

Only now can I understand why Marianne would spend so much time picking out the perfect doll for our little girl, Anna Marie. Then when the grandchildren came along, it was the same. Not just a doll, but a special doll with the most real-looking face and dressed so pretty. Yes, it's probably a lot to do with that stick of wood wrapped in a rag so many years ago. Was it adversity? I think it was, because a neighbor actually burned her doll in the yard with the trash on purpose. A day she will never forget. The scars of childhood never go away. Did good come from the adversity? Oh, yes, no telling how many pretty little dolls passed through her hands to create that smile and first hug on a special Christmas doll. Who received the most out of this childhood trauma? Well, St. Francis said it's only in giving that we receive. So there were many blessings in every doll.

My childhood was good as I look back on it. I had fun and we were happy. I was asked to join the cub scouts and went to the meeting at the den mother's house. Then there was a time when we needed a uniform to identify you as a cub scout. Well, it was very expensive for the Moodys, so we started with the cap. As time rocked on, that's all I ever got. We would be asked to show up at places in full uniform, and all I had was my cap, so I soon lost interest in this. As you could see, I felt a little out of place. I had no problem with this because the boys began to talk about all the activities the scouts were to be involved in later on. They would get to go camping in the summer. The more they talked, the more I realized my dad was doing all these things with me. He would take me hunting with him when I was very small. I still remember on a cold winter night sleeping in an army tent on a cot with all those quilts Mama had sent along. After the big bonfire had died down where the hound dog had been sleeping beside, he would ease in very quietly and curl up on my cot at my feet. That was OK, matter of fact, it felt pretty good.

While we are on this camping story, let's expand it a little. This camp was in the Ocklawaha River swamp in the Ocala National Forest. That's where we spent every day and weekend during hunting season we could. The hunting, hearing the dogs run, cooking on an open fire, sleeping in the tent, it was just the most fun of a small boy growing up.

The question might come up, "Was God there watching over me all that time?" I believed in Him, but didn't spend that much time on where He was out there in the woods.

One day there were two brothers, one about my age, maybe eight or nine, I don't know for sure, and one smaller, maybe two or three years younger. I don't even remember who they were or if they were cousins or not. Anyway, we got tired of hunting all day with the grownups and decided to stay at the camp and go fishing. First order of business was to get some worms. Have you ever grunted up earth worms? If you haven't, you have missed out on another of life's most exciting times. You drive a stob or a board in the ground with your ax. Then with the ax or a brick you rub it across the stob or board in the ground so it will vibrate. Now you might have to keep driving it in a little more until you get just the right pitch of vibration. When you get it right, and if you have picked the place where the worms usually live, here they will come crawling up out of the ground. That was more fun than going fishing, I believe.

Well, we got the ax and found a hole of water where

the ground was damp and started clearing out the vines for a clean place to grunt the worms. I was chopping out the vines, and the two brothers were cleaning out the leaves and trash. The older brother would hold a vine, and I would chop it off. We were just about finished, and I was coming down with the ax on one more vine when I saw the older brother reach out for a vine. My ax was already coming down right for his head. It is as clear now as around 70 years ago. It was going straight for the top of his head. I slid my left hand up the ax handle toward the ax head to try to stop it. He wasn't looking up, so he didn't know what was about to happen. I managed to stop the ax as it touched the top of his head, just enough to break the skin. Of course, he grabbed his head and his little brother saw this and thought I had split his head open. He got so scared and just took off crying and running through the woods. Yes, I was between a rock and a hard place. I had to see how deep the cut was first, and after finding out it was only about an inch long and not deep enough to bleed, I started out through the woods to catch the little brother. So, I did catch up with him, and explained it was not bad at all. I brought him back and all was well. I guess I should mention we never did go fishing or get any worms.

Now let's go back to our question – was God there watching over us boys in the woods back then? You can bet your life He was. I was not mature enough to be doing what I was doing with that ax. Just suppose I didn't see him reach out in time. Just suppose my hand didn't get all the way up the handle in time to stop it. Just suppose it had gone another inch or two right in the exact top and middle of his head. I would have ended his life right then. His brother would have that tragedy to live with the rest of his life. I would have that guilt to carry to my grave. One fraction of a second would have impacted the three of us forever.

Yes, God was there looking after three little boys and giving us another chance at a normal life. Life would never have been the same.

Thank you, Lord, after all these years for looking after us when we can't see danger for ourselves.

We did a lot of black bass fishing in the St. John's River when I was coming up. When I got old enough to cast a rod and reel, my dad bought me a little casting rod about three feet long. As I recall, all reels then had the crank for your right hand. Well, since most people are right handed, they would cast the bait with their right hand, change hands to hold the rod in the left hand, and bring in the bait or fish with the right. My dad said, no, when the bass lure hits the water is when the bass is usually going to strike. If he sees it stop and sink a little while you are changing hands, you will probably miss your chance. So I had to learn to cast with my left hand and have ever since. Some children I took fishing this week noticed and asked if I was left handed. So I told them the story. By the way, that little rod is out in the garage now.

If we had two or three hundred yards of shoreline to fish, we had no trouble catching enough fish for supper. I can still see a little bug like a very small mosquito hawk with thin wings, lighting on my paddle. I still have no idea what its name is. Then I would say, "Grandpa, what is that?" "Oh, that's a 'vanagery', " he would say. Grandpa was living with us now since Grandma died, so whatever he said I took as Gospel. I guess it was many years later I was to learn that whatever kind of bug I asked about and he didn't know either – it became a "vanagery."

The paddles were always so big for me as I tried to move the boat down the shoreline for my dad. So Grandpa made me a small cypress paddle, just the right size for me. I was sick in bed with the flu or something when he was finishing it and could hardly wait to see it. He even took a piece of broken glass to scrape down the wood to put a smooth finish on it. When he finally finished it and brought it in the bedroom, I was one proud little boy. A paddle of my very own. It stayed right on my bed till I was well.

Such fun after school to rent a boat from old Gus

between East Palatka and San Mateo and paddle along the shore. Of course, we didn't have an outboard motor, or "kicker" as they were called. That was for people who had real money. After lunch you could rent the boat for 50 cents at the half-day price.

Nowadays, at my age, some evenings I'll sit in the rocking chair on the porch and tell Marianne I'm about out of gas. Seems that expression has taken on a little different meaning. Know what I mean?

Now this little part is about me as a small child. But keep in mind I'm not trying to convince you that the old days for me were the best. I'm speaking "old days" like when you could go to the little country store, get an R.C. Cola and a moon pie, give the kind man your ten cents with no tax. Then have plenty of free time to go outside on the bench or under a big oak and just enjoy every single bite. Just makes your mouth water, doesn't it?

As you might know, these times "back when" had other meanings to many folks. That ten cents was not always available in your pocket. If it was hot when you got that R.C. you went outside where there might be a breeze 'cause there was no air conditioning in the store. Or sometimes it was cold and there was not enough heat. Now and then the trips were longer on foot when there was no car. There was wood to get in and splinters to chop. There were vegetables to gather from the garden and crab grass to hoe. There were clothes to hang on the line after Mama washed, beans to can in the spring, and leaves to rake in the fall.

So you see, I'm not saying these were the best years, but I've been there and done that and just want to share it with you.

Lord, don't mind the mule, just load the wagon.

CHAPTER 3
GROWING UP - MY DAD, MOM, AND ANN (My sister)

I was born in La Crosse, Florida, on June 11, 1934. La Crosse is a small town about 15 miles north of Gainesville, a farming section of Alachua County. Still today as I tell folks where I was born, it's easy to tell if they have ever heard of it before. If you were from there or in the area, it's La Crosse, with a long a; if not, it's La Crosse with a short a. Very simple, but very true to this day. There were two stores; my uncle Fred had a small grocery store in the middle of town, and Mr. Roberts had another on the opposite side of the road down a little, and as I remember, his had more dry goods. My dad had a filling station and garage a short distance away where he sold gas and worked on cars. I can remember that old gas pump with the glass tank on top with the numbers from 1 – 10, it seems like, going up the side of the glass. There was a big lever at the bottom to pump the gas to the top of the glass tank, and you would stop pumping when you got the amount of gallons you wanted, and it ran into your car by gravity. Of course, some of you might remember this and some might not. Boy, what fun it was when they would let me pump a little bit. This was the time when I was about three years old, 'cause by the time we eventually moved, I was four.

I guess another of the exciting things about La Crosse was Peggy and her regular trips through town. We had a big packing shed right beside the railroad tracks where she picked up the local produce from the farmers, to be taken to the larger markets. Oh, I guess I forgot to mention who this Peggy was, didn't I? She was our local steam engine for the freight train. Now she wasn't just the train, Peggy had personality; everyone around knew her and when she was coming. Even the crew that worked on her was a little different from today's railroad men. Of course, there were times when they were short of coal and would have to stop and gather some wood along the track to help make it on. Now in cane grinding season when syrup was being made, the engineer would stop the train so the crew could buy some syrup because everybody had to have a quart of new syrup, that was a must. I guess times were just different back then. Can you remember when the first diesel trains came out? Maybe not, but all the steam engines were black, and the new diesel engines were purple. So, as you might guess, she was now Purple Peggy.

My sister Ann started to school there and, of course, remembers more than I, for she was seven years older than me. There was only one small school, and I remember Mama telling us about going to a play there one night and my Uncle Herman went along. Part way through the play, Mama said he slid down in his seat and said, "it's kinda like cold coffee." In other words, it was not his favorite. I don't remember my sister and me fighting much – we got along pretty well, being there was so much difference in our age. I do remember when we were washing dishes, she would wash and I would dry, and she would want to sing "In the Garden" and try to get me to harmonize with her. Oh, I did try, but after a line or two, I'd be singing the same as her. Then we would start all over. That hasn't changed a bit. I still can't harmonize any better now...but I can wash dishes, though!

Then there were fun times at Georges Lake, a big lake in west Putnam County. In those days, as I remember, there were no houses on the lake at all, and now they are side by side all around it. We would take Dad's boat on an old homemade trailer, and as soon as he pushed off from the bank to fish, Ann and I would swim on the sandy shore until he came back. Then he and Mama would start a fire in a "coal pot," as he called it. This is a cooker made with fire brick material and covered in a thin metal. I've never seen one since I grew up. He "put coke on," as he called it, for fuel. It was charcoal, made from burning slabs from the saw mill and smothering the fire out so they would not completely burn up. This he bought from some old man close to home. I never knew anything about buying a sack of charcoal. Then on went the big frying pan, and the bass he had just caught for a fine fish supper. Such fun we had at that lake as kids!

Then there was my Grandpa Moody's house, just down the road from the packing shed. He would always tell his wife, "Anice, you are going to burn the house down." She always put much more wood in the heater than he would. So it was one day when he got home from a preaching tour to see his home just a pile of ashes with nothing left. All the folks had gathered around to see what Mr. Moody would say when he returned. As he gazed on the pile of ashes he said, "The Lord giveth and the Lord taketh away, blessed be the name of the Lord." What a response to losing your home. I wish I would be remembered as such, but I'm afraid I would not have thought of that line.

Well, Grandpa needed a place to live, so a short distance away was an old Methodist church that had been closed down for its age. Grandpa believed he and Grandma could move in it and use it for their home. I guess it is like a little old saying in the newspaper called "Hambone" that my dad would read every day – he said, "Half of something is better than all of nothing." Grandpa bought that old church and moved in. Now mind you, this was all before I was born. The church was abandoned for its age before I was born, and I was 76 this summer. Wood was good back then, wasn't it? I went by there within the last year, and people are still living in it. The only thing different is a small air conditioner window unit on one side.

Grandpa's House

Here's a story I just have to tell you about. When I was very small, Daddy would take me deer hunting with him lots of times, and I would stay with my grandpa on the roads and Daddy would take the deer hounds and the car to put out the dogs. We would just hang out on the road because I was too small to go in the woods. Grandpa always had a half-pint whiskey bottle in his overalls pocket for a water bottle. It was getting hot one day, and Grandpa said we needed to walk down the road to the branch and fill his water bottle. It was just a few feet down to the water, and I got me a drink and filled his bottle and handed it up to him. He turned it up right then like he was really thirsty. I looked up and I can see it as if it were yesterday – that little tadpole swimming for his life upstream in that bottle. Just as I hollered out "GRANDPA," the little fellow disappeared through the neck of the bottle. He takes the bottle down real quick and asks, "What?" I said, "Oh, never mind." I didn't say anymore and neither did he. Some things are just better left alone, don't you think? Since we'll have forever, I'll just tell him about it someday.

My dad's brother, Herman, was also a Baptist preacher and a farmer. Times back then were really hard, and his old car had given out. My dad had bought a Model A truck for $50 after we moved to Palatka just 'cause it was a good buy. He put it in the back yard, and I played in it, pretending I was driving and shifting the gears. Dad, in turn, gave the old truck to Uncle Herman so he would have something that would run. There were no doors and a wood body on the back, but it did run. I went over to see Uncle Herman's son, Pete, and stayed for a few days. Pete was a couple of years older than me, but we always enjoyed playing together. Just guessing, I probably wasn't but about eight years old. They had the old Model A running by then. Well, it was the night Joe Louis was having a big fight. This was big news in La Crosse. Maybe you don't remember Joe, but what a boxer he was! Joe was a big, powerful black man and well respected by all.

He held the world heavyweight championship from June 22, 1937, until March 1, 1949, when he retired.

He was the son of a mentally ill sharecropper. After his mother remarried and moved to Detroit, he began the U.S. Amateur boxing. Then he went to Golden Gloves titleholder with 54 fights; he won 50 and lost 4. His first professional fight was on July 4, 1934. So Joe Louis was a big name in the boxing news even for us kids. I remember it being said that "Age was the only thing that would claim his title." I guess it proved to be true.

Anyway, Uncle Fred had a radio at his store in town about two miles away. As far as we knew, that was the closest radio. So, Uncle Herman let Pete and me take the truck to the store where a group was gathered to hear the fight. Joe won his fight, and I can't remember who the loser was. We didn't have any lights on the old truck, but it was a bright moon out, so we started home. Pete let me drive part of the way, and I just remember crossing old Peggy's tracks. I am going to try to explain this as well as I can. The gas pedal was a metal rod coming up through the wood floor with a round top on it about the size of a 50-cent piece. After a few minutes running, the gas pedal got very hot, and of course, we boys didn't wear any shoes, so what a problem that caused. I can still remember putting my big toe on it, then sliding over my foot to try another spot, and so back and forth like holding a hot potato in your hand. Only you had to keep the gas pedal in the same place so the old truck wouldn't keep speeding up and slowing down. Well, so much for my first time driving in the moonlight.

Our family moved from La Crosse, Florida, to Palatka, Florida, in 1938, a move of about 60 miles. My dad got a job as a state food inspector with the Department of Agriculture.

This move from La Crosse to Palatka was a big thing for the Moody family. For one thing, it was in the depression, and my dad would have a steady pay check from the state of Florida. To have a regular pay check in those days was something to be very proud of. I can still remember hearing them talk of envy and jealous words from family members because of this. I still don't know how my dad heard about the job or who helped him, but I remember Mama saying he borrowed enough money to buy a new suit and went to Tallahassee to apply for the inspector's job. I'm assuming my dad had to see the commissioner of agriculture himself to get this job. This was Nathan Mayo, the state's first commissioner of agriculture, and one of the governor's cabinet. As I recall the stories as a kid, Mr. Mayo approached the state about being their commissioner and enforcing the laws, rules, and regulations for mainly what people ate. It covered all stores that sold food and the buying and selling of all food products. Later, it was expanded to cover weights and measures and selling gas for your cars. So the state told Mr. Mayo they could not afford his services and a department as he wanted to establish. He then offered them an agreement to raise enough money by the passage of a law to put a tax on each 30 dozen cases of eggs of four cents. By doing this, the state could raise enough money to start the agriculture department at no cost to the state. The people would pay for him and his workers. He also said if he failed to raise enough revenue to be self-supporting in the first year, he would quit his job at the year's end. The state officials agreed and the first commissioner was a success. I do not know what year that was, but soon after, this became an elected job, so Mr. Mayo was out campaigning for election. He came through La Crosse and stopped by our house to see my dad about helping get votes in Gainesville. He also ate dinner with us while he was there. My sister Ann, being seven years older, remembers Mama buying a new plate to serve him sliced tomatoes on. The story was passed on to me that when they went to Gainesville, Dad and Grandpa took me with them. I was less than four years old, and Mr. Mayo held me in his arms and taught me to say, "Vote for Mayo – he's a good man." So I guess we can call that my first campaigning job.

THE STATE OF FLORIDA
DEPARTMENT OF AGRICULTURE
TALLAHASSEE

NATHAN MAYO
COMMISSIONER

June 22, 1955

Mr. Doyle Moody
P. O. Box 204
Palatka, Florida

Dear Doyle:

I want you to know that I appreciate very much your good letter of June 11th, and I want to congratulate you and your wife on Doyle Benny Moody, junior. I trust he will grow up to be as good a man as his Daddy is, and his grandpa and great grandpa whom I know, and knew, quite well.

Yes, I remember the day when you were a little fellow, when your grandfather (I believe it was) had you in Gainesville, and I took you up into my arms and we made quite a campaign trip down the street.

It was very thoughtful of you to write me.

With kindest regards and best wishes to you and your Dad, I am

Yours sincerely,

Commissioner

NM:aws

Mr. Mayo's Letter

After the move to Palatka, my dad had seven counties around our county of Putnam to inspect every grocery store. Later on with much growth in Florida, it was cut to five counties. You can believe me when I say that there were many people trying to cheat the public back then just as there are today. There had to be laws and someone to enforce them. Some of you might remember the old scales that were used mostly in the meat department. It had a horizontal drum that rolled as the meat or whatever was put on that scale. To look at the sight glass in the scale with nothing on it, it read zero as is should; however, if the inspector put on it a one-pound weight from his kit, it might weigh 18 ounces or so – more than it should. Sometimes, the store owner would paste a coin on top of the drum and as it turned down, the gravity on the coin would pull it down farther than it should. So, there was much money to be made on a penny or a nickel on the drum. Of course, when the pork chops or whatever was taken off the scales, the coin would roll to the top and the sight line would be back on zero as normal.

Then a sample of eggs had to be looked at under a bright light to see if they were fresh. This was called "candling." I learned that there are about seven thousand air cells in an egg, so air can get in to spoil the freshness. Now, they seal each egg, and it stays fresh much longer than in the early days. The word "fresh" on many food items was not allowed.

When I was in my teen years, I remember some meat companies were using a product called sulfite to mix in with hamburger meat to turn it very red and look much leaner than it really was. I'm not qualified to explain what the chemical composition of sulfite is, but I think it is used in making fertilizer. I do remember when some workers found this out, they took a sample of the hamburger to Tallahassee and rubbed it on the corner of their boss's desk. It took the finish right off the wood, so it didn't take very long to get this procedure outlawed. So then all hamburger had to be tested.

When I was in high school, almost all country grocery stores sold kerosene because it was used in so many homes for heaters in the winter. This was also one of my dad's new jobs - to check each kerosene pump in his five counties to be sure the public was getting a quart or a half gallon or a gallon on the three settings that were usually on each pump. So Dad paid me a little each week to ride with him on his route and check these pumps, correct them if they were wrong, and put a state seal on it when I finished. I did this while I was out of school for the summer and before we opened the grocery store, so I was not in high school yet. It took me almost the three months to do this in the summer. By the time I left home and got married, I knew his job almost as well as he did. He died of a sudden heart attack with a short time to go for retirement. The commissioner of agriculture at the time called me and asked if I wanted this job and said they would hold it open for a while so I could make up my mind. I called them back after a few weeks and said no. I was in the paper mill by then, married, and with one small child. I would have had to take a pay cut, and I didn't want that. As well as I can remember, his salary was a little over three thousand a year with an expense account and mileage for car allowance. Looking back, I think I figured the total wrong. When I figured it out, it was too late. Also at the time, I just couldn't see me dealing with the public and so many people, plus it was very political. I was definitely not a politician. "Vote for Mayo – he's a good man" was about my last venture into that area.

As I matured, I came to love people, their lives, their stories, so I would have done well in the job. I still don't like politics to this day, but feel like this would not have kept me from doing the job well. One of my best friends in school asked for the job and was hired right away. He did well and retired long before me. As I look back, I believe it was one of the worst decisions I ever made. Only God knows. I ended up working 23 years of shift work and never enjoyed a bit of it. I was probably looking at the paycheck and not thinking about what my dad had taught me. He said, "Never hold a dime so close to your eye you can't see a dollar a little farther out." So, if you hold a dime in one hand close to your eye and a dollar bill in the other hand, the dime will block out the dollar. Good lesson. I also have learned when we are offered something and want something else, God sometimes says, "Just go ahead, my child, and learn for yourself." I had 23 years of 8-4, 4-12, and 12-8 shifts to think about this, and I still do.

Another little story I want to mention about Mr. Mayo is a story he told at his retirement party. With his age and his failing health, the state of Florida held a large retirement party for him, and all of his employees were there and, I'm sure, many more friends and family. My dad wanted me to ride with him to Tallahassee for this, and I'm proud to say I was blessed to be there. Mr. Mayo told of the days before his state work and about owning a grocery store in mid-state. If I recall, it seems that his brother was in the business, too, but don't hold me to it. Anyway, he explained how it was that you bought an item, resold it for a profit, and that was it. So, he came up with the idea that if you bought a large amount of an item (food, we are talking about) so as to get it for a cheaper price, you could sell much more because folks would purchase more of it. He then decided to buy a train car full of rice. Now that was a real venture for a country store owner in those days. They repackaged the rice in smaller bags, maybe 10 pounds or so, I don't remember the exact size, and put their cheaper price on it.

Then he also decided that if he could somehow let the surrounding area know about this rice sale, it would be even better. Now in those days, there were cars, but not everybody had one. Many people were still walking down the dirt roads and some paved ones to get to town or wherever they needed to go. I remember Mr. Mayo explaining that if a person was walking down the road and saw a piece of paper lying in the road, he would stop and pick it up to see what it was. Can you imagine someone doing this now? So, he and his workers at the store wrote that he had so many pounds of rice for sale at such and such a price. They put the sale information in an envelope with his name on the outside and made a large stack of them. They then took them in a car and drove down a long road leading into town, throwing them out along the way. The next day I believe, one of his friends came into the store and said, "Mr. Mayo, somehow you lost all your mail on the road and I picked it all up and here it is." Of course, he received a big laugh from the crowd gathered, but he went on to explain that that was his first experiment with advertising. From what he learned with a carload of rice, he later used to advertise the state of Florida for the tourist industry. We know now that this is a very large industry. Many thanks to Mr. Mayo and his rice sale.

I have one last story from the vice president of a very large grocery store chain in the state. He explained first that he had a red-haired wife and he tried very hard not to cross her in any way, if possible. Being a normal man, he had his pet peeves, too. One of them was having his coffee spilled in his saucer when it was being poured for his breakfast. However, sometimes his wife would get the cup a little too full and some would spill in the saucer. But learning from the past and moving to the future, he drank his coffee, ate his breakfast, and didn't say a word before leaving for the office. Now one time he got to the office and his day was not going so well, and his secretary was waiting to hear his first instructions of the day. The poor soul – she got all his frustrations all at once that had built up since the first drop of coffee ran over the rim of the cup in his saucer. Of course, the vice president got all his anger out on his poor secretary that couldn't be released at home.

This man closed by saying to the many inspectors that would be entering their stores in the future to please keep this little story in mind because just maybe one of his store managers might have had his coffee spilled in his saucer that very morning.

You see the words that could come after that between the state of Florida and a huge grocery store chain could be a disaster. This would be all because of an attitude of one person.

The lesson I learned from this is to try to be careful with what I say in response to another's words that I don't necessarily agree with. We might try first to seek why they said it or what caused them to say it. I don't always remember, but I'm trying.

My dad's job was centered around Palatka, so in June of '38 he stopped at Angel's Dining car and got us a hamburger as we got to town. It's still the best burger joint around. I got one for lunch just last week. Sat at the same table I did as a teenager with my friends or my date. I would soon realize that date would turn out to be my wife, Marianne.

Then when I was in grammar school, he bought a third of a block between Main and Madison Streets and bordering Fifth Street in Palatka, which was 100' by 300' for $350.00 of unpaid taxes. That was to be our garden for many years to come. During World War II, the government encouraged anyone who had the space to start a victory garden. Times were hard and money was short, but my mom knew how to handle life like that. She had been raised very poor, too, so we were in good hands. When the garden came in, she knew how to can the fresh beans and tomatoes, so in the winter months we would save on the grocery bill. I remember she would boil the quart jars full of beans in a large pot, then take them out and give me a table knife to run down inside the jar to get all the air bubbles out. There couldn't be any left, it could cause the beans to spoil and go bad later. It was a boring job, but she knew how to teach me what was important and what was not. She knew about hard times and how to handle them. All of our clothes were ironed so neatly with an electric iron. You see, this was a big improvement from her childhood, heating those heavy metal irons on the wood stove or by the fireplace. Did she complain? No, this is life, and you learned to deal with it one day at a time. Thinking back now, she probably didn't see it as hard times with hot and cold running water, electric lights, and stove, kerosene at first, and indoor toilet and three-bedroom home that cost $2,000.00. She was coming up in the world.

After Grandma died and Grandpa had a heart attack, he moved to Palatka and lived with us, and helped in the garden. It wasn't long before Grandpa was sitting under the live oak tree selling fresh vegetables to the neighbors. When Daddy planted peas or beans, he would open the top of the row with a hoe, wet the ground good from a flowing well that was on the place, and then I got to walk barefooted down the row to mash the seeds in the wet dirt. Boy, what fun! I can still feel that mud coming up between my toes. Then he would cover it with some dirt. It had to be just so deep, and little boys didn't know about those things.

Now this garden I've been talking about was what I did in the afternoons and Saturdays. You probably had your chores, too. I learned a lot about life in that old garden, my grandpa on one side of the row and me on the other. When our hoes would touch and made that little sound of two pieces of metal touching, Grandpa would always say, "that means we will hoe together again someday." Who knows what he meant, that's all he ever said about it. Maybe someday he and I will be helping raise food for those heavenly banquets. It's a nice thought, anyway.

Me and Grandpa

In the middle of our garden was about an inch and a half flowing well that I mentioned. No telling what used to be there. It was great to have all the water we wanted to raise the garden with good pressure in the well so we didn't need a pump. On top of the well was about an inch and a half tee with a metal plug screwed in it. So to water, all we had to do was stand behind the well, unscrew the plug, and a huge stream of water flowed through the dikes and over the garden. Now mind you, when it came time to shut it off, it was a different story.

Daddy and Grandpa had a piece of old tin about three feet square that they got behind to put the cap back on. I was much too small for this. Of course, when they got the cap in front of the four-foot stream of water and tried to put it back on, it was a sight. Even trying to stay back of the old piece of tin they would get very wet sometimes. Finally, after much ado, I could see the huge circle of spray getting smaller until it was capped. Not for a minute did I ever think to say, "Dad, let's put a valve on it!" No, that's just the way he did it and I thought it must be right.

I can see now in my older years why children get the wrong message and go astray. Dads aren't always right, but as little children, we think they are. My dad wasn't teaching me the best way to shut off that water; he was teaching me his way. I can see myself now doing things the same way he did, not necessarily the best way.

As I look back now, I'm sure my whole family has wanted to say many times, "Dad, why do we have to do it like this?"

Then before you know it, Santa gave me a nice bicycle with a basket on the handlebars, and I was in business. Fresh beans, squash, corn, peppers, okra, and cucumbers were delivered right to your door. I would come home from school in the spring and early summer, pick a basket full of vegetables out of the garden and start knocking on doors in our neighborhood. They all knew me, so it usually didn't take too long to sell out. The housewives were all kind and nice to me. I can also remember our bell pepper being such a good crop I had to go to the grocery store or market. I'll never forget the first trip on the bicycle to Mr. Taratus' grocery, The Groseteria. He looked over the nice big peppers I'd picked and said, "OK. I'll pay you 50 cents a bucket full, on consignment." Boy, that was a big new word. After he explained what it meant, I agreed – well, actually, I didn't have much choice. It turned out good though, and I learned a lot.

Compared to what he paid for the bell peppers back then, they are up to a pretty price of $1.29 each now. So you can definitely see the price difference between then and now.

In the second grade, my teacher heard me talking about my garden and ordered a bunch of collard greens. I was so proud, going to school early and waiting for the teacher. Sitting on the sidewalk with all the collards you can roll in a newspaper. I had enough in there to feed an army. When she gave me my 10 cents and thanked me, I felt like a real businessman.

When you get retirement age, you tend to look back at the special times as a child. Nowadays, who knows what the youth will look back at – a huge amusement park, Disney World, a trip to the islands, who knows? One thing I'd like to tell you about my childhood that was really special was a cane grinding. Some of our kin folks had farms and would invite us to come. Just to watch that powerful old mule walk around in a circle pulling the long timber that turned the cane mill and then they would let me stick a few stalks of cane in it. Boy, all that sweet fresh cane juice running out at the bottom where you could just help yourself. There was always a piece of burlap bag (we always called it a "croker sack," don't know where that name came from) to strain it a little. There was always a cup or something to drink the juice from right out of the mill. Then, of course, getting in on watching them pour the green cane juice off in the big open kettle with the hot fire under it to boil it down for syrup. You might as well know right now of all the fancy pies, cakes and sweet desserts in the country, new syrup, homemade buttermilk biscuits, and homemade butter is the best there is. There is just nothing to compare it with – makes my mouth water just writing it down. I always remember after my meal, I'd eat several biscuits and syrup, and then on what I thought was my last, I'd get too much syrup and have to have one more biscuit to clean it up, you know, to make it come out just right.

Like any boy, I had to have a jug full to take home,

and after a day or two in the refrigerator it would pour out in long strings and had gone bad. I would be so disappointed, but it just wouldn't keep at all. Even before it went bad, it never tasted the same as right out of the mill, with all the fiber from the cane running down. Those were the days.

One last mention of the juice fresh out of the mill. The word of God is fresh for us daily right out of the Bible. It's good, it's refreshing, it's exciting, and most of all, it's nourishing.

You might be like me and like to read other books by good Christian authors about their stories and opinions of what the Word says, and that's good. We hear lots of good messages on tape and on the radio, especially, as we are driving. We hear others preach at church and talk at Sunday school on their interpretations of the Bible. I am here to say it should not take the place of reading Scripture yourself.

Again, it's like the cane juice fresh from the mill – that's when it's best. God's word is fresh daily for us. It hasn't been changed, watered down, heated or cooled by others – just fresh from the mill as the cane juice.

Lord, don't mind the mule, just load the wagon.

CHAPTER 4
WHAT I LEARNED IN SCHOOL

Maybe I'll say first what I didn't learn so good. Reading was hard in grammar school for me, so I never read well later on, and this was the reason for me not to read books when I became an adult – and here I am writing one! I'm sorry for that. I've just got interested in reading in the last year. Another weak place in school was spelling, and I'm terrible at it today. After my writing gets cold, I can hardly make it out myself. I'm blessed with a friend who says she is going to help me with this.

Now for what I did learn. My dad had two kinds of recreation: we hunted deer in the winter, and we fished for bass the rest of the year, and that was it. So when I got big enough to go camping with him (I guess about 5th or 6th grade), he would go to school and get the teacher to give me my lessons to make up ahead of time and get permission to take me out of school for the first week of hunting season. I killed my first deer, a small buck, at the age of 10, in the sixth grade.

So when I got to high school and was driving on my own, a week was out of the question, of course, but I did want to be in the woods opening day.

I well remember walking in the principal's office the day before the season opened. Back then it was always on November 20. There were two boys ahead of me. The first had a long sad tale of why he just had to be off the next day. When he finished, Mr. Eastham said very kindly, "I'm sorry, that won't be an excused absence. Next." The other young man had a different story; I don't remember what it was, but he had to be off the next day. He got the same answer: "Sorry, but it won't be excused. Next." I knew I didn't have a chance, but I was already in line, so I might as well give it my best.

I simply said, "Mr. Eastham, my dad has taken me out of school on the first day of hunting season since I was in grammar school. It opens tomorrow, and I would sure like to be there." He signed me an excused slip of paper and handed it to me, then he turned his head to the first two boys who were still standing to the side and said, "See what telling the truth will do for you?" I learned one of the biggest lessons of my life that day and have tried to use it ever since. Be honest, tell the truth, no matter the cost. Sometimes it may be embarrassing, but not nearly so much as trying to tell several lies trying to cover up the first one. Besides that, if it's one of the big 10, it must be important: Thou shalt not bear false witness.

Next lesson – I have always been short. I guess the only time I was considered big was when I was born and weighed eleven pounds. I was a big baby, and have been small ever since. So my short sleeve shirts seemed to always come down to my elbow. I had a class after lunch somewhere about the 8th or 9th grade. I don't remember what it was, but as soon as I sat down, the girl behind me would turn up my shirt sleeves a turn. It didn't matter to me, but it bothered her, so I just let her help herself. Well, this went on the whole year. I soon got used to it – as a matter of fact, very used to it. I just couldn't stand that shirt down to the bend in my arm. What am I getting at? Here I am 65-plus years old, and I still have to turn my sleeve up a turn. If I'm going to church, out to eat, or whatever, the habit is still there. When we are forming a new habit, we don't look down the road 50 years, do we? We don't say, "I'll turn these sleeves up if she wants them up and later just forget it." Habits don't work that way. We might say, I'll have a few beers after work with my friends or smoke this or that with them; we won't always be together, and later I'll do what I want, maybe even stop altogether. Or maybe my friend, my trusted friend, says "Here, take this little pill just this once and see how it makes you feel. If you don't like it, you don't ever have to try it again." Someone tells an off-color story or joke and you laugh and see all the others laughing, and then remember one you had heard. You see all the attention they got for their little story, so why not try yours? Then one leads to another and so on. I've been there and tried it; don't get hooked, telling off-color jokes doesn't lead to anything good. Stop a habit before it gets started. Some of them seem harmless, and some will cost you your life. It's not that simple. Sometimes I put on a shirt and think, "I'll be the only one there with my sleeves rolled up and nobody will know why," and of course, they never ask. (Take a moment right now to look at the photo on the book cover. In a mad rush to get this picture taken, I actually forgot to roll up my sleeves! It was the very first mistake that I saw, and it was too late to change it!) Think about this the next time you are starting to do anything that can be a daily habit. If it's a good one that will give glory to God, stay with it. If it's not so good, be careful – it could become a daily thing (50 years later).

The next lesson came in the 9th grade when I took typing. It didn't seem like a hard course and a lot of my friends were taking it, so why not. Well, as it turned out, it wasn't so hard, and I can't remember any homework, but to tell you the truth, some students are cut out for typing and some are not. Guess which group I was in? Right!

I do remember "now is the time for all good men to come to the aid of their country." I guess if we taught that today it would have to say "men and women" – life was much simpler back then, wasn't it? I have no idea why this was the sentence we had to type every day when we got to class, over and over, and then we got into timed typing. It was hard enough to type and hit the right keys and not make any mistakes, but now Mrs. Warwick wanted us to see how many words we could copy out of the typing book in a minute without making mistakes. Boy, the pressure was on. I found that when you are trying to beat the clock, the mistakes sort of skyrocket. Then the classmate next to you is doing so much better, and that adds a little more to the situation. Now that you got a little better with the one minute, not good understand, but a little better, she comes up with the five-minute timed writing. Man, what a mess. When I would get my paper back with all those red marks on every mistake, it was a sight for sore eyes. I can still see a little red slash on each wrong letter.

Five minutes – whoever heard of typing five minutes in a row without stopping? By now I am saying, "Bad choice, Doyle, you should have picked some other course."

Back to the lesson in this. One day my history teacher, Mrs. Carter, who kept study hall also, asked me to deliver a note downstairs to Mrs. Warwick, my typing teacher. When I walked in the room, she was sitting in a student desk at the back of her class with her back to me. Just as I walked up to her, I saw she was grading papers, and you'll never guess whose it was. That wasn't hard, was it? When she finished with all those little red slash marks, she moved her pencil down a bit and wrote a big 39 with a ring around it. About then I broke the silence and handed her the note from Mrs. Carter. She took it and looked down at the paper and back at me and said, "Doyle, is that the best you could do?" I said, "Yes, Ma'am, the very best I could do." She crossed out the 39 and over to the side she wrote 83. I thanked her and I left. I left to go back to study hall with one of the most important lessons of my life. Always strive to do the best you can at whatever you are doing. I passed typing that year, not on my grades, but by doing the best I could do.

I took her a box of candy at the end of the school year. I still remember her husband looking kind of surprised as I handed it to her. I'm sure he didn't know about the lesson of 39 to 83.

I guess I learned a lot more in high school, but these three lessons are some I use almost daily.

How about you? What did you learn or what are you learning that's really important when you get my age?

I'm not promising you all your 39s will turn out to be 83s, but I will assure you that in the school of life, you will not fail if you will strive to do the best you can at whatever the task.

Lord, don't mind the mule, just load the wagon.

CHAPTER 5
THE EARLY YEARS OF MARRIAGE AND FAMILY

After graduation, everyone back then wanted to go to the beach, of course. I can't speak for the girls, but the boys wanted to go because that's where the girls were. Simple as that.

My friend, George Willis, and I decided to rent us a hotel room at Daytona Beach and stay a week right after school was out. I always had a little money in my pocket. My dad and mom had a grocery store and I had been working since I was 13, every afternoon and all day on Saturday. Well, actually, I swept it out before school, too. The pay was good; I made $5 a week at first, but later got raised to $7.50. So, I could afford to go to the beach for a week.

Moody's Grocery

The high school sorority girls did the same. Rented a house on the beach and had someone's mother for a chaperone and off they went, too.

The first night, George and I go to the boardwalk on Daytona Beach where all the fun was. We walked by the Ferris wheel, and right on the very top seat, coming over my way was a very pretty young lady with coal black hair, who I remember taking a geometry class with, even though we were two grades apart. She was 16 and I was 18. We spent the whole year of the class together and never spoke to each other. Why? Who knows. Anyway, when I saw her face on top of the Ferris wheel, I knew she was the girl for me. When the ride stopped and she stepped off, I was waiting for her and have never gone out with another girl since that night. She graduated two years later, and one month after, we were married. Fifty-seven years ago, the best thing that ever happened to old Doyle. Sounds like a fairy tale, and I guess it has been and still is. I have so much to be thankful for.

My dad heard of a little house for sale out in the edge of town. It was on the highway, a good location for us to start out. So, he helped me make arrangements to get a loan from Federal Savings and Loan in Palatka, and I started buying the house before we were married. The house had two bedrooms, a living room, kitchen, and bath. Twenty-four feet square was the entire house. About the same size as our living room now. I don't know how we did it, but we were so proud – it was our mansion. The total price of the house was $4,250. Somehow, I scraped up $1,250 and borrowed $3,000 on the house. Now, I would have to get used to those big house payments – yes, $33.00 a month. I could handle it, though, for I had a better job now. My first job after I got out of school was with an asphalt paving company at $.85 an hour. So, if I made a week, it was about $34.00 before taxes. It always rained us out some, so we never made many full weeks. Now with my new job at the paper mill, I was making $1.38 an hour. Quite a raise. Life is usually tough on young married couples, but if you really love each other, you can make it. Maybe God's plan is to let you go through those times so you will be experienced enough to withstand whatever lies ahead in life. I don't think we knew times were hard; it was just the way life was, and we were happy.

When Marianne and I first got married, we would come to St. Augustine and eat at Marty's. A dozen shrimp was $1.40. You could go to Pappy's and get the same for $1.25. The shrimp there was good, too, and everybody knew Miss Maude, a nice old lady about 70 years old, who was the cashier. Also, at Pappy's you were served iced tea in a quart canning jar. But we were young, and for the extra $.15 we wanted a little more class. Oh, I'll have to tell you this, as soon as we got back off our honeymoon, I wanted to take my wife to the finest place around. We went to Marineland to the Dolphin Restaurant, a huge buffet, anything you wanted (including sardines) for the one price of $2.50 a person. Boy, was that up town for us! I do remember, at the time, we had $35.00 to our name. I guess we were poor, but we didn't know it, and here we are living just one-half mile past where that old restaurant was almost half a century later.

With the children coming along soon, we were a happy little family. They played in the sand under a small tree in the front yard or we sat with them in the front porch swing. One summer I made them a small pool about three feet wide and five feet long out of a few cement blocks I had. With about a foot of water in it, you just can't imagine how much fun they had.

We would even cook a steak now and then on a piece of chicken wire over a bucket of charcoal, or we would make homemade ice cream in an empty Crisco can. I had made a handle on top with a piece of wire so we could twist it back and forth in the dishpan of ice and rock salt. You had to open it once in a while and scrape the sides down where it would freeze first. Boy, what fun! My mom said Grandma Davis, her mom, used to make it for them when she was little. They always had a syrup bucket with the handle already on it to use. Of course, it was just on special times back then when they could get some ice, Mama said. Ice came on a wagon from town and had to be stored in a hole in the ground lined in sawdust and wrapped in burlap bags. These are special stories!

With the children coming along, we soon needed another room. With the help of my dad and my good friend, Goose Graves, we put on a little bedroom on the back for us. There were many happy times "out on the hill," as we called it. We also bought two extra lots later on. I think the price was $250.00, so now we had room for a big garden. (This was where the highways 19 and 20 cross.)

When my dad died suddenly of a heart attack in 1961, we moved in with my mom to take care of her. She still lived in town where I was raised. I can't remember how long it was after that, one night I asked Marianne if she heard that noise; it was the neighbor's light switch. I said this is just too close, we are going to move out of town.

We had already bought some property in East Palatka to raise leather leaf fern. An old fellow in that neighborhood had died and left his home. I went over to buy his boat and motor, and his brother told me if I would buy his place, he would give me the boat and motor. It was a small two-bedroom house with 100' of riverfront, and he wanted $10,000.00 for it. We finally bought it and sold our little home on the hill, built another bedroom, and fixed it up real nice. We moved on the river about 1964, I think.

Any of you that have ever raised one or several knot head boys that are always in to rough and tumbling in their playing will relate to this if a little girl comes along. Anna Marie and Gary were only fourteen months apart, so coming up when they were little, they played together well and were very close. What I want to explain is the big difference when the boys were playing and she would crawl up in my lap with that long blond hair, fine as corn silk, with her doll. Girls are special in a different way. The feeling I had at that moment, with her just sitting there in my lap – words on a page just can't do justice to this, I'm sorry to say.

Then if Dad needed her, she was ready to help. Let me explain. When we bought the house on the river and added on to it, we decided we wanted hardwood floors in the dining room, living room, hall, and the new bedroom. We had hired Marianne's dad, Pop, her grandfather, and her uncle Harold to make the additions, but we ran out of money, and I had to finish as best as I could

I had never put a cut nail in a piece of tongue and groove oak flooring in my life. This was in the days when oak flooring was buying bundles of oak boards in various lengths from maybe 1½ feet to 3 feet, nailing them to the subfloor with square-shaped cut nails in the tongue side so the next board would cover up the nail. Being this was the third time this old house was built on to, it had a long narrow living room. I would start down that thirty-three foot long room on my knees and think that I would never get to the end. Then I felt such joy when I did get to the end and realized I'd added about 2½ inches to the width. Marianne's folks had told me about putting soap on the cut nails to help a little in driving them in. I needed all the help I could get. It helped in the effort and in the oak not splitting as bad. Anna Marie is 52 at this writing, and was too young to remember this. We were still living in town and I would bring her and Gary over to the river house with me now and then. Ben was in school. I would give them each a bar of soap and show them how to rub the nail in the soap and lay it along ahead of my work. I can see her now down on her knees, with that long blond hair hanging down, rubbing those nails in the soap. As a tiny little girl, she was always ready to help Dad, and that hasn't changed over the years – she's only willing to help more. As she matured and grew, she became the peacemaker in the family. Whether it was her family, our whole family, or friends, she used her God-given talent as a peacemaker. Matthew 5:9: "for they will be called sons of God." Now, we enjoy worshipping with her every Sunday in our church. What a blessing!

We really enjoyed living on the river and bringing up our children there. It had a big enough yard to play in and plenty of fish in the river. Once again we were well blessed.

I can still see Gary out in the sand pile outside the kitchen door down on his knees having fun with his trucks. It was just after his first crew cut. Marianne always had cut all our hair, but this time decided that Gary needed a crew cut. Very short. He would play a little, then reach up and run his hand over the top of his head to feel that short hair. Then he would play some more. Some pictures just stay in your mind, don't they?

Another thing I have learned is that you cannot back up time. Now and then, early in the morning when we didn't have to go to school or church, I would feel Gary slipping in beside me in the bed. He wouldn't say a word, just lie beside me very still. After a short time, I'd say, "Well, if you go put on my coffee water, I'll get up." I can tell you now that if I could go back to those mornings, I would lie there a lot longer, and enjoy the comfort and closeness of my child. I write this down to say how sorry I am for getting up so soon and also so that you might think about some precious moments you might be missing. The remembering does not go away.

When Gary was little, we pretty well knew he would never make a living with his hands. It would have to be with a pencil or his head. How wrong can we be. As a very young boy, he wanted to drive a semi truck down the road. So he found a man to teach him and let him drive his truck a little. Then he wanted to learn how to run a bulldozer. He did the same way and learned to operate a big machine on his own time. I don't think he got any money for learning to operate the truck and the bulldozer. Then he went into the pulp wood business, welding, some farming, and he has been using his hands ever since. It seems like the challenge with Gary is if you can do it, I can learn to do it, too. I might add that if I need to know where a certain story is in the Bible, I can call Gary and he will usually know where it is.

I have another short one about Gary. I've always enjoyed going floundering in the inland waterway at night to stick us a mess of flounder with a light and gig. One such night, just Gary and I went. He was old enough to run the boat motor, so he would put me where I wanted to pole down the shore. It began to get late, so Gary put a boat cushion under his head and went to sleep on the back seat. I remember calling him to change sides of the river. He would jump right up, crank the motor, take me across the river, lie back down, and go right back to sleep, all in a few minutes time. Such fun we had!

Another night, it seems like the whole family was in the boat, and at the mouth of the creek, Gary stuck a big flounder. The fish started moving out to deep water with Gary trying to hold him on the bottom as best he could. I reached and grabbed his overall straps just before he was about to fall in.

Going floundering was a fun time when the children were small. Of course, I'm sure they all wanted to go home long before I was ready. I would stay in the front with the gig and leave Marianne and Ben to keep the boat straight off the bank in the back. There would always be plenty of small ones, and whoever saw it first would say, "There's a small one," and I'd say, "But he will make a sandwich, oh, well, we might as well take him home, too." So, to this day, all small flounder in our family are called "Oh, wells." The example being we might go fishing and catch three nice flounder and two "Oh, wells." I'm just remembering those fun times.

Ben, the oldest, had to learn fast, do more, and be ready for what was next. When we had our Friday night Bible studies at the Ticknors', he was the babysitter. With our three and at the time their five, Ben was the teacher for their Sunday school. He did well and kept them quiet for our Bible study. Of course, when he asked who did the whale swallow, and Anna Marie, raising her hand said, "Pinocchio," his patience did get a little short.

He would go with me red bass fishing when the others were too little. It was always a rush after work and before it got too late, so his job was to make as many wire leaders as he could before we got to the beach. Fishing in the rocks, across from where we live now, a lot of times you hang up and never get your sinker and hook back. He was too little to fish, but he sure got some good training in leader making.

Since we had this three and one-half acres of shade land there within 200' of the house, I decided to try to raise enough leather leaf fern on it to make a living. Sure was getting tired of shift work at the paper mill.

We all had to cut fern, and the kids hated every minute of it. Seems like it was too hot or cold or there were mosquitoes or something, but it was no fun, I'll tell you. At that time, $100 per week was very good wages for a family. In good fern, you could make $100 per week per acre, so I figured we had three and one-half acres of land, and we should have no trouble making a good living at home. Wrong. It never did work that way. The cost of living went up faster than the price of a fern leaf, which was about two or two and one-half cents per leaf.

Because of their hard work, we did manage to pay off our home early and afford to eat out every Sunday and things like that. For the five of us at San Mateo restaurant eating shrimp, the bill was $13.50. Of course, that was living very high on the hog.

Looking back at that part of our life, I will never be satisfied with my decision to grow the fern. I wanted to work for myself and be my own boss, and that was OK. The part where my children had to work every afternoon before they could do anything else still bothers me to this day. I don't think it was fair, and for this I am sorry. I'm not perfect, and all the decisions I have made in life haven't always been good ones, but looking back will destroy you. So, I'm trying to learn from my mistakes and look to the future. May God bless each of them for their labor.

We had a big birthday party once a year because two of the children, Ben, the oldest, and Anna Marie, four years later, were born on my birthday, June 11. When they were small, there was no way Gary, who was born on April 21, could understand all those birthday presents and him not getting one. This was before Keith came along. So we just wrapped up one more gift, and Gary had two birthdays a year for a while.

Keith was a very small child when we were winding up the fern cutting. He had a coonskin cap that he loved to wear, complete with the coon tail hanging down the back. So one day, Marianne was cutting some fern and had Keith along with her. When she started to leave, he walked away from her and pointed ahead saying, "Pretty hat, pretty hat." She had no idea what he was talking about, and he just would not come on with her so she went back a few steps to look. There in a patch of fern was a huge diamondback rattlesnake coiled up ready to strike. Marianne grabbed Keith's hand and pulled him back just as he reached for the snake. The coloring of the snake looked to him like his coonskin cap at home. Thanks be to God that she got to him just as he tried to pick that snake up!

Looking back when the other children were bigger and leaving home, Keith, our youngest, was left there to take their place. So when something needed doing or I needed another hand, most of the time we called on Keith. The other three had to work very hard in the fernery as young children. So now, as I had quit the mill and lost the flower business, it was his turn to help. He had fun on the river with plenty of fish, and he learned how to be a good fisherman at a very early age. Now he can out-fish me any day and open a cast net better than I ever could. I remember him and his little friend jumping off the dock and swimming in the river, having so much fun. I looked at the water when they came out, and there was a very large gator on top of the water right where they had been playing. Another thank you, Lord. There was no more swimming in the river after that.

Things were tight at home after we lost the truck and I took on the cookie route. All summer, Keith had to roll out of bed every morning and help me run the route. Money was scarce, and he knew it. We ate a lot of out-of-date cookies and broken packages. I remember telling him to open a certain kind going down the road one day and he said, "Dad, you mean open a new package of cookies?" That was unheard of! Then when we lost that job, Keith and I had to mow some people's yards for a while to make ends meet. He never complained and did a good job as best he could at his age. Before he left home, he put in his hours, too.

We have covered a lot of ground in this chapter about starting a family. There were fun times and we lived off what we made. I can never be thankful enough for the help of my wife and my four children in helping me with whatever I needed in these slim times.

On one of our family trips to the mountains in Linville Falls, North Carolina, we stopped for gas and the rest room at a small country store somewhere in Georgia. This was before I-95, so we were on a two-lane state road. When I was paying for the gas, I remember asking the lady what in the world all that crowd of people were doing out there in the far corner of the cornfield. They were right out in the open on a hot summer day. She said, "Oh, that's some peanut farmer who thinks he's going to run for President." I guess Jimmy Carter started out the hard way and tried to reach the average person as a voter.

Lord, don't mind the mule, just load the wagon.

CHAPTER 6
WHAT I LEARNED IN THE PAPER MILL

Most of my working years, as I have told you, were in a paper mill. One of my last jobs in the mill was being responsible on my shift for all the chemicals that it takes to bleach the wood fiber to make white paper. The four chemicals were chlorine, caustic, hypochlorite, and chlorine dioxide. The area was set off by itself because of its danger. The control room I worked in was a very small brick room with walls about two feet thick for protection in case of an explosion from making chlorine dioxide gas. The good news is that we had only one such incident ever. The bad news is, guess whose shift it was on? Praise God I didn't get hurt; I just ruined my clothes due to the sulfuric acid raining down on me.

I had many hours alone in that little building. As a matter of fact, I just remember I was reading the paper just back from vacation when I heard that loud noise, and I didn't even jump up, thinking it was a fellow worker with a cherry bomb trying to scare me. What a surprise then, trying to close off twenty-three hand valves as fast as possible under the rain of a mixture of acid and other chemicals. By the way, that's been thirty-five or forty years ago, and I still have a dream now and then and close off those twenty-three valves and in the exact order they had to be closed in! I just wish my old mind would help me out a little more with such things as, "What's that new couple's name that came to church last Sunday?" Or, "I just laid my screw driver down a while ago, and now where in the world is it?" Know what I mean?

During these days of working in the paper mill, I remember one time I was on vacation and we were staying at the beach. All the family wanted to stay as long as we could and use up every minute of the beach trip. I was to start the 4-12 shift on my first day back. Well, instead of packing up the day before and coming home the way we should, we stayed until the very last day. We packed up that morning as fast as possible and piled all our week's stuff in the boat hooked up to the back of my old Jeep station wagon. Seems like there was even a rollaway bed in there with our clothes, and all the food we hadn't eaten. By the time we got it all put away, the time was really short for me to make it to the mill in Palatka at 3:30 p.m. We still had to go by the house, leave all this, and get me to work. So, Gary and I took the Jeep and boat full of stuff and headed out, and Marianne was to finish and come on in the other car with the other children. Well, when we hit the end of the old wood bridge across the Matanzas River, I was going too fast for that little dip at the end of the bridge. Also, the boat was loaded much too heavy. There was just too much against us. That one bounce, and the trailer hitch came off the ball. I looked in the rear view mirror just in time for me to see the boat and trailer rolling over in the road end over end, sort of like a football on the ground. I can never do this scene justice, but with all the fishing equipment, bed, food, and clothes, it was a sight to see. I turned around and drove back. Gary and I got out and walked up to this big mess as best as I can describe it.

Now let me tell you what this little fellow taught me. He was maybe four or five years old. One look, one sentence. "Daddy, look. Our watermelon is busted all to pieces." Yes, that's what his little eyes saw. Not a boat and trailer upside down, beds, food, and Lord knows what else. Our watermelon we didn't eat is gone now.

You see, he was teaching me that everything is relative. What my eyes see and your eyes see may not be the same. What is a disaster to some may not be so bad to others. All I could see was my boat and trailer and the boat motor. I didn't think about all the time it was going to take to get home and get to work. All Gary was seeing was that big old long green striped watermelon. Yes, I can still see it.

Now for the lesson. When we are listening to someone's problems, it's oh, so easy to jump right in and say, "Oh, that's not all that bad. Let me tell you what happened to me the other day." They know right off that you are not listening to their troubles. We need to stop and look and listen through their eyes and ears. It may be a life-changing experience to them at the time, and to us no trouble at all. The next time a friend or family member says, "I'm at the end of my rope, it's just terrible and it can't be fixed," remember the boat and trailer and all the mess, and among it all a big, green striped, busted up watermelon.

Well, you won't believe it, but we loaded it all back up, hooked up the trailer, and it had very little damage. We got it all back home, and I got to work a little late, it seems like. Hard to believe the damage was so light. All except the watermelon.

Getting back to what I learned in that little brick room. I had a friend that worked just across the railroad tracks from me. I had a chemical he needed on his job, so he would call, and I would turn a pump on, so we were in touch every shift. Sometimes when things were slow at night on his job, he would come over and chat a short while. Through these little visits, I learned that he was a true atheist. Well, it just so happened that I had always wanted to talk to someone face to face that did not believe there was a God. It did take a while for him to agree because he was very touchy about this. Later he agreed to come over on the three-to-eleven shift, and we would talk – one time. I was excited for the chance I just knew was coming to talk to a real live atheist and help him see the light and explain the Gospel. I had my Bible on the little desk where the report sheets were lying when he walked in.

I will never forget his first words when he saw it lying there. He just said, "That book was written by men and I don't believe it is true, so don't even open it or talk about anything in it." Next, he was ready to hear what I had to offer.

The main part of my story ends right here. I didn't have anything to offer him but faith, and he wasn't interested in anything but facts. As you might think, this conversation didn't last too long. As far as I could tell, he didn't learn anything, and on my end, I couldn't see that I had taught him anything.

I do not remember if it was this very night or just close to it, but he told me he was buying a motorcycle. Well, he was no young boy, so my next words were, "Are you ready to die?"

His response was, "Don't talk like that." I explained that I felt his chances were greatly increasing. He did get his motorcycle, and he lived three more weeks. He had a wreck and died at the scene. What a shock to me feeling, "Oh, dear Lord, if only I could have made a difference." The only glimmer of hope he left me with is, sometimes he said he would go to a church on Sunday morning and sit on the back pew "just to see if anything would happen."

I wish I could end the story with more for you, but I did learn that it's not as easy as you think it might be. Sharing God's word with others is not always simple. It does not always work as we planned. It is our job as Christians to try, and not trying is a failure. Simple as that. I did try, and oh, what a story it could have been if he had been receptive!

Moving on to the next little story, I learned in the little building about a good friend that was an electrician on my shift and actually had lived close to me when I was a teenager and he was a young man raising his family. He was such a fine man. He was born in Poland and came to this country after World War II. I had heard about him being a holocaust survivor in Germany. As you might know, I sure wanted to hear his story. I asked several times, and sort of like my non-believer friend, he didn't want to talk about it. Then one day, he said, "OK. I'll tell you one night when work is slack." He would come by and talk, and when the pulp mill needed an electrician, he would get a call on his radio. There was only one thing he asked, and that was that after his story I would never ask again and we wouldn't talk about it anymore. I gladly agreed.

He was in the army fighting against Germany and was captured. He served time in Auschwitz and Buchenwald both, but I don't remember in what order. He told me when they were on the train and being moved, he saw these tall smoke stacks with smoke bellowing out, but he had no idea what was going on inside the buildings. One of his jobs turned out to be a pretty good one, and that was taking care of Adolf Eichmann's horse. Remember him? He was one of Hitler's right-hand men. Then later on, he went to the work camps to grow food for the armies. The men in charge of these work camps would work the prisoners with very little food on the farms until they died. Each morning, a horse and wagon would come by to pick up the ones that had died during the night. There would be others, too, because sometimes when they would wake up, there would be bodies hanging from the rafters. I guess it was suicide or a way of getting rid of certain ones. He told of being afraid for his life all the time. He told of watching them drag the lifeless bodies to the door and the guards holding arms and legs and throwing the bodies on the wagon in big piles.

Then, his day came, and he was thrown on the wagon, but he happened to be on top of the pile. Before the wagon pulled off, a guard saw him make a slight movement. Of course, being unconscious and near death from starvation, he was told this later. The guard called out, "That last one isn't dead yet – throw him back down." And they did. That guard had some compassion someplace in him, and saved his life.

About all they lived on were a very few boiled potatoes. The guard would give him a few of his potatoes for an extra portion, and eventually nursed him back to health. I'm sure God is hard to find in a place like that, but my friend found His grace did exist in one of Hitler's death camps. They were surrounded by a high electric fence, so because my friend was an electrician, he was chosen to get the tools to cut the fence for an escape. They planned it all, and did get the fence cut. A group got out and ran a short distance to the woods. Then, they heard a loud shout from the prison to come back because the war was over, and they were safe. By the grace of God, there was a happy ending to a terrible story. So, when I hear stories about the holocaust and see pictures of the starved prisoners, I can picture my good friend and his story, which I never mentioned to him again. We were friends for many years after that.

Have you ever been afraid? I'm sure most all of you reading this can answer yes. Now I don't mean when your brother or sister jumps out in the dark and yells, "Boo!" I'm thinking more like have you been in a life-or-death situation and been afraid for your life. We have talked about sad times, happy times, good times and bad, but now we are going to mention a scary time.

As you might know, the first of the four bleaching agents in those days was chlorine. We used a lot of it. There were two tank cars hooked up at all times. We pulled out of one and had the other ready when it ran out. A car lasted about three days. Each car had a separate track, so the train crew could change cars at any time and not affect the one being used. This story takes place about two o'clock in the morning on a very foggy night. The train crew made a mistake in the heavy fog and coupled up to the tank car we were using. After moving the tank car only a short distance, they saw the line break and the chlorine pouring out, so all they could do was unhook it and move the engine and crew as fast as possible. I'm really not sure how I found this out or whether I just came out to get a sample to run. Maybe I had heard the lines break, but anyway, I recall looking toward the chlorine dock, and it was a sea of green fog. The chlorine gas was about chest deep. It was an awful sight to behold. In this much chlorine, you will die in seconds.

I ran back inside to get my Scott air pack on. A gas mask won't do any good in this much gas. The air pack is like firefighters use, with a face mask and an air tank on your back. We had practiced many times putting it on, but as I recall, no one had ever had to use it. So many straps had to be airtight, and I was in such a hurry. Now comes a choice: I could run in the direction the wind was coming from and save myself, or stay and try to save the several hundred people in the mill. I didn't have to think about it at all; my personal safety was not in the decision. I must save these workers. I finally got on my air pack, turned on the valve to breathe, and eased out in the chlorine gas. It was like wading out in a green lake of water, because you could see nothing from the chest down. The chlorine car was beside a cement platform with steps that led up to the side of the car. Now the car is equipped with a check valve just like the one on a water pump. If a line breaks, it will check and stop the flow of gas. But when the train unhooked, the lines just had a kink in them, so the gas was not full force, and the check didn't work.

The next part I remember in detail. I got on the catwalk on the side of the tank car, and the broken lines were hanging down from the top and across the catwalk, with gas pouring out below. As I eased under the metal pipes, they hung up on my air tank, so I just stopped for a second. I remember very clearly saying in my mind, "Doyle, if you let these pipes catch your air valve on your back or let it pull this face mask to one side, you are going to die right here." I was so scared, and breathing so fast I would not have been able to hold my breath long enough to run to safety. So, I remember talking to myself to stop, to take my time. There was absolutely no room for a mistake now. I reached toward my back, lifted the pipe a few inches off my air bottle, and got under it. Then I climbed up to the top of the car and cut off the main valve. That was a glorious sound, hearing that chlorine stop. I got back inside, and the gas had not filled the little room. I took off the mask and made one phone call to the bleach plant on the top floor so they could relay the message to the rest of the mill. Look at the smoke stack, go into the wind, and it will clear shortly. By then, my friend and bleach plant operator, Bob Hayes, came down and helped me put the air pack back on one more time. I needed to go out and double check everything to be sure everything was off as it should be. There are 3,000 pounds of air in the tank and it should last twenty-three minutes, if I remember correctly. I walked out the door and ran out of air. When you are scared, you use up a lot of air in a short time. On the first bottle, I was outside ten minutes at the most. If it had given out on top of that chlorine car, that would have been the last of old me. I probably didn't have over two or three minutes of air left when I got the valve shut. God is good.

The lesson I learned was, self-preservation always speaks very loud, but sometimes you must put others ahead of yourself.

I received lots of praise, letters from the company, and pats on the back from my fellow workers. Most of all was the blessing that I helped save the lives of many workers that night.

Lord, don't mind the mule, just load the wagon.

CHAPTER 7
A NEW VENTURE

When the children started leaving home, we soon found out we couldn't take care of the fern by ourselves and there didn't seem to be a living in it now, with no more land than we had.

I had about 21 years of shift work in at the mill and was still wanting to work for myself. I still remember the clock going off for me to go in on the graveyard shift from 11 – 7. I sat up on the edge of the bed about 10:30 and told Marianne I just couldn't do this anymore. I had to find another way to make a living. In the next few days we talked a lot. She said we could open a flower shop in the old grocery store building my mom still owned. Flowers have been her lifelong hobby and she is good at it. She could probably make a broom handle sprout if she stuck it down in the yard and watered it a little. Me, I hardly knew a rose from a petunia, but to get off this shift work I could learn. We had fun fixing up the old building like we wanted it, and finally got the shop open. Marianne was in her heyday, buying and selling plants and flowers of all kinds. Of course, there was a lot of visiting that went on and that was fun, too. We found that most people that like flowers and can grow them are very nice people and fun to have around. After two years, we were making enough in the shop for me to quit the mill, and it was a joyful day. Here we were working together and doing well.

This brings to mind a sermon I heard many years ago by a priest named Miles Cooper, a quiet gentle man. He said the one thing everyone can count on is change. Nothing ever stays the same. Sooner or later there had to be a change, and change it was. Palatka was a little quiet one-horse town when here came the big boys. Along with shopping centers come plants, too. They could sell them for less than I could buy them, so you can guess what was about to happen. We had made many friends and had given good service with free delivery, but it wasn't enough. We always kept some nice potted plants for gifts, funerals, birthdays, and the like, and put pretty paper, a bow and a card, then delivered it for just the price of the plant. Usually, it was about one-third of florists' prices, so the customer got a good deal. We always kept an assortment of small pots of African violets in full bloom and found them to be a good seller. Then with times getting tougher, our customers wanted us to wrap, put a bow and card, and deliver a $2.95 violet for a gift. Then we started getting in a smaller size of violet we could sell for $1.50 (they were a good item), but you guessed it, they wanted them wrapped and delivered, too. That was hard to take.

Marianne had been in the cake business at home for years, baking and decorating birthday and wedding cakes, and, of course, for any occasion. Like a master carpenter with a piece of wood, she could build anything with cake icing. Since every cake was a homemade pound cake, there was no need to advertise. At every wedding, they would take a bite of cake and ask, "Who made this cake? When my daughter gets married, I'll know who to call." If it was a five-pound birthday cake or a thirty pound, four- or five-tiered wedding cake, it was all pound cake. With that many cakes you know one would fall now and then, and boy, would we have a feast!

Back to the flower shop. With business getting worse every week, we were depending more and more on the cakes to feed us. So now, it was me in the shop and Marianne at home baking cakes. Going broke very fast. Such a change. Lord, what are we going to do now? When I quit the mill, I had one thing in mind: I wanted to be home every night and be off every Sunday to go to church. Well, we were able to go to church every Sunday and I was at home every night, but money was in short supply, I'll tell you. We had only one boy, Keith, in school. The three older children – Ben, Gary, and Anna Marie - had already moved out.

It makes me think of how Anna Marie and I would be cutting fern together when she was little, maybe around 10 or so, and she would say, "when I get married I'm going to have so and so." Already thinking about her wedding and reception. I guess this was because we delivered so many cakes and saw so many weddings.

Anyway, I would laugh and say the same thing, "Honey, I'll be so poor by then all you will probably have is Kool-Aid and bologna sandwiches." We laughed and joked about it as she was growing up. But you know, that big day does come, and I never forgot. Marianne had made her a big beautiful tiered wedding cake with all the trimmings a daughter could want, and right in the middle of the table, old Dad had a quart Mason fruit jar of grape Kool-Aid and two bologna sandwiches. Wish you could have seen her face when she saw the table! Someone got a picture at just the right time. It still makes me laugh. Of course, she had kinda forgotten things like that, but when she saw that table it all came back.

Now, on a more serious note. Do you know when you really learn about life, about love, about what really matters about who God really is and see His face? It's when times are tough. It's when you don't have the knowledge or the wisdom and don't know where to turn next. I had to do something. With very few customers, I decided I had enough free time to build some crab traps, and since we lived on the river, could catch and sell a few live crabs for a little extra income. Crabs were up to around seven dollars a bushel. That would be some good money coming in and would help us in these slow times. I could run the traps after work out in front of the house and be in before dark. Sounded like a good idea. (By the way, I just talked to a commercial crabber in July, 2011, and he laughed at the seven-dollar-a-bushel story. He said he sells them for $50 a bushel, but they are $60 to $65 a bushel in town. My, how times have changed!) We wouldn't have to invest much. I bought a roll of plastic-coated wire and some hog rings and the pliers to crimp them and was in business. Every day, I could cut out the wire and build the trap in the quiet times in the shop. Maybe this would help. There seemed to always be a good market for blue crabs from the river. Now for the bait, we had to have some kind of fish. To buy fish, probably mullet, the cheapest, cost money, or you could catch them yourself for free and with a little work, of course. I had this old gill net I had bought for $25.00 from a friend. It was a good nylon net, with plastic corks, and a good lead line, and about 200' long, seems like. Well, if we could string this out in the river and catch river mullet for crab bait, it wouldn't cost us anything. I got that out and you never saw such a pile of tangled lines in your life. It had been in a box for years. We tried to untangle it in the yard and got it full of little sticks and trash, and it seemed to get worse. Well, the next move was to get in the river and untangle a little at a time, maybe that was the way. The alligators weren't so bad in those days. I wouldn't be at ease in there now, for there are just too many.

Now comes the lesson I learned, so slow down and read this carefully. Late one summer afternoon after closing the shop, we took the net to the river bank and started untangling the lines and moved further out as we pulled the net behind us. What a mess it was! It was just before dark when I looked across the circle of net and saw my wife in neck-deep black river water, frantically working at the net. I will never, never forget the picture. It's still in my mind. I never did doubt, but that afternoon, Marianne really loved me. She loved me just for me, 'cause by then I had absolutely nothing to offer.

Do you take this man for better or worse? Her "I do" was serious. She meant it then and has every day since. Marianne has stayed by me and encouraged me in all our bad times and all my failures; she has been right there, neck deep in dark water. It would be much nicer for all concerned to read it on a pretty Hallmark card, put together in a meaningful poem. My friend, let me tell you, that day, I knew my wife loved me and always would.

I have no idea who will read this or how long it will be before they do, but if you are married or someday plan to be, think about this little story and say to yourself, "would I do that for my mate?" When you answered "I will" or someday when you answer, does it mean neck deep for my loved one? Will they mean it when times get rough? And you can bet times are going to be tough for all of us. I pray, and you should, too, that there will be a mate for you like the one I have. Thanks be to God! I believe hard times make strong people.

Lord, don't mind the mule, just load the wagon.

CHAPTER 8
THE DAY I KNEW

Sometimes we struggle with problems and do what we think is our best, and then, there are times when it seems as though it's just not good enough. The day came when I knew our shop, The Flower Patch, wasn't going to make it. It was an hour or so before closing time, and I called Marianne at home to tell her I had taken in a $20 bill, and what should I bring home for supper. When I hung up the phone, I knew we were beat. There was no way out, no way to fix it, no money to change it. Maybe you have been there. If you haven't, take it from me, it's a scary feeling. I don't remember what I bought with the money. All I remember is the $20 bill and the phone call.

In the last chapter, we talked about the crab traps and the net. I must confess, all I ever got out of that venture was the afternoon in the river in neck-deep water. Looking back, that was enough. We never caught any bait and never got any crabs. One thing I knew was that I was not in this alone; Marianne was with me.

About this time we were chosen to go on a three-day Christian weekend called "Cursillo." Cursillo means a short course in Christianity. Well, what could it hurt at this time in the game; we were so depressed, anything might help. So we said we would go. Someone, knowing our condition, arranged for the weekend to be paid for, otherwise we could never have gone.

The men were to go first and the women to go the next weekend. I well remember Marianne telling me when I left, "You have three days to think about this situation, so when you get home Sunday night, tell me something." Meaning, what are we going to do. I know now there is a whole world full of good people, God-fearing people, going through this kind of thing all the time. You know what? When it's you, it feels like you are the only one with these troubles, you just can't see anyone else's. Have you been there?

I did go and I did come home Sunday night with the very last answer she ever wanted to hear. I remember her saying, "Well, what have you decided?" My answer being, "Nothing, really, but from here on I'm not really worried about it." You can believe it or not, but that didn't go over real well. I received something on the weekend that assured me if I would put my trust in Jesus Christ, He would take care of me. Not that everything would be rosy; there would still be rough roads ahead, but somehow I knew God would work it out.

The next week was a long one. Marianne was really worried about what we would do next, and here is old Doyle saying, "Don't worry about it." Walking around smiling like a kid with Dad holding on to his overall straps so he can't fall. We made it through the week, and she, too, came to realize we would make it somehow.

I would like to add a short word about the Cursillo movement. I have used its Christian message and worked in it for around 30 years. I had the privilege of meeting the last living man who helped start it in 1942 in Spain. He gave a talk in Jacksonville some 20 years ago. I was preparing to give a talk to a group of men in the near future and asked for some key words from him. He paused a few seconds and said, "Usually when men get together they talk about what they know or what they have, but not about what they are. In Cursillo, we get together because of what we are, to explain how we should be and then how we are going to get there." (This was from Spanish to English, but this is the meaning of his advice to me.) I was blessed to be there and talk with this humble Christian man.

Later, my oldest son, Ben, called the shop for a little information. He was a mechanic, and a good one, at the Pontiac dealership in Palatka. Seemed to have a good job, had been married about a year, but was getting tired of pulling wrenches. You know the feeling. Said maybe he needed a change. This friend had been coming by for work on his car and telling Ben about the trucking business. He and his wife were seeing the whole country, having a good time, and getting paid for it. It just so happened they had another semi they wanted to sell. (Don't laugh now; wait 'til later.) So Ben calls me to tell me he is just burned out at the mechanic job and wants a change. He tells me about this tractor and refrigerated trailer the people owned and had a driver hired to drive it for them. The money looked good on paper, every trip showing good profit. What he wanted to know was, how do you go about borrowing $38,000 to buy the rig?

Let me explain it this way. Have you ever been hungry, I mean starving – you go into a restaurant and the girl hands you a menu with two or three dozen choices of every kind of food you can think of and some you never heard of. She's standing there tapping her pencil and saying, "What'll it be today?" You don't even feel like reading all those combinations, you just fold the menu and say, "Hamburger and fries, please." I just bet you've been there. That's about the way it was with me. I didn't have time to shop around for a new venture (or look at the menu), I needed something now.

Yes, when Ben got through telling me about this venture he was planning, I said, "tell you what – how about me calling around for the money and going in with you on the truck; we'll do it together." He knew I had to make a change quick. Of course he said, "Let's do it." What a change from a mechanic to a truck driver and what a bigger change from flower shop owner to truck driver.

I first called the credit union where I had banked all my working years at the paper mill. Since the credit community and board of directors were made up of the men I had worked with for years and years, it didn't sound like there would be a problem at all. I just prayed, "Lord, if this be your will, let them lend us the money and I'll know this is the sign." Now, it seems the president of this credit union was a very sharp old banker and didn't know Doyle and Ben from Adam. Besides that, he checked into the trucking and said loans on big rigs were a bad risk. I went to his office and tried to change his mind, but he said no. I even told him about praying and he was not impressed at all. Now to Plan B.

The owner said if we could come up with $10,000 cash, he would finance it himself. No problem. We could borrow $5,000 each and be out of Dodge before you knew it. Of course, word got out fast, and my friends found lots of nice ways to say, "You're crazy." I told them all the same thing: there is a little bit of adventure in all of us. In a short time, we had the down payment and the paperwork was done. The plan was for Ben to quit his job to coincide with the truck coming to Florida to pick up a load. The driver lived in west Florida and had agreed to stay on and train Ben to drive. He figured that would take about three weeks. This would give me time to close our flower business and get rid of the floor stock we had.

Everything was happening so fast, a lot had to be done in a short time. You know, I don't even remember thinking about asking God to give me that sign. If the credit union approved the loan, I would know it was the right move. Too bad, Doyle, too late now.

The date was set by phone and the truck was to come through Palatka about 10:00 p.m. on a certain night on the way to Miami. The big night finally came, and we met Ben and his wife, Melony, at the filling station.

One big green Kenworth. Man, what a truck!

We met the driver and had a little small talk, but the time was tight, as we were to learn later. Ben had his bag packed, and it was time to tell his wife goodbye. We wished them well and left, so they could say their own goodbyes. She was not happy about all this. I sure couldn't blame her.

Going home that night, we were busy talking about what was next. We had to move fast. I had to be ready to go on the road after his three weeks or so of learning to operate that rig.

Lord, don't mind the mule, just load the wagon.

CHAPTER 9
THE PHONE CALL

We had only a few miles to drive, so when we opened the door at home the phone was ringing. I picked it up and Ben said, "Dad, the driver just quit. After you left, he called his wife, and she said if he would catch the next bus home she wouldn't leave him; otherwise, their marriage was over." It didn't make sense then, but it does now. He said, "I have to leave for Miami in about 30 minutes, are you going with me or not?" Probably the most earth-shaking phone call of my life. How many things can you think of in the next ten seconds? Three weeks was going to be short of time, but 30 minutes? Marianne agreed that we didn't have a choice. We couldn't let him do it alone. I know you can't, but try as you may, it was about 15 minutes driving time back to town, trying to think: what do I need to take in as small a bag as possible to be gone for Lord knows how long. We were running around the house getting some clothes, razor, towel, wash cloth, toothbrush – I could hardly think. Those few minutes are still not pleasant to think about. It was a single sleeper cab, so I couldn't take much, as space was really tight. Marianne said she would do the best she could with the business. This seemed to be another time she was in neck-deep water. Bless her heart. She drove me to the station with a handful of things in my bag. Ben and Melony were waiting.

Now, you need to understand what we were facing. Ben had done some work on a big rig for a friend and had to leave it parked on the street for him here in town. At this time, he had never driven one at all. He said he had to leave his place, get the truck turned around and headed in another direction to park on the street. All this was in less than three miles. So that was his previous driving experience.

As for old Dad here, my other son, Gary, had a temporary job with an old semi and had asked me to ride with him one night (in the passenger seat, of course), about 30 miles, to pick up a load of potatoes. That was the only time I had ever been inside the cab of a rig. These things I was thinking of as we drove up to that big green Kenworth with a 360-horsepower Caterpillar engine and a 40-foot refrigerated trailer. Lord, what have we got ourselves into? He could have said, "Remember the prayer you prayed" – but he didn't, matter of fact, he was very quiet that night. I probably couldn't hear him over that Cat engine, anyway. I remember asking Ben if we could get this thing out of town, and he assured me the driver had gone over the 13-speed gear pattern with him, and it was also on a sticker in the top of the cab. (Don't laugh now, it gets worse.) The driver gave us our address to pick up a load of shrimp the next morning in Miami, some 350 miles away, so we had to hurry. We said our goodbyes again and eased out of town – I might say, scared to death. The driver told us not to forget to stop at all weigh stations, loaded or not, and anything we needed just get on the CB radio and a trucker would help. Ben is a fast learner, so he did well at finding those 13 gears, and out of Dodge we rolled.

The Truck

By this time it was on into the night, and the load was to be picked up early in the morning, so we didn't have much time to molley around. The first order of business was to find the next weigh station, 'cause we didn't want to run past it. We had all the trouble we needed for the time being. When we got on the radio to ask, they said something about a "coop," we thought. What do you suppose a coop is? We wanted to find the scales. Of course, as we would learn very quickly, a chicken coop is the scales where the trucker weighs his chickens – slang for his load, whatever it is. We found them all and didn't run past a one. We even made it to Miami on time. Can you remember in the early '80s, a place in Miami called Liberty City, where they had all the riots and fights and fires? It was like a war. Well, that was our address, and the only building standing on the block was the fish house. All the rest was burned to the ground. Then we had to back up that long trailer. Boy, what a trip! It was nothing like a boat trailer, I'll tell you. We did manage to get it backed in place, and it seems like by mid-morning we're loaded and had our papers to deliver.

I'm going to close this little short chapter here for a reason. Remember the phone call? I'm afraid you'll forget if I go on. I don't know if you have ever received a phone call like that. I don't know if you have been that confused after getting a message, a very unexpected message. I'll tell you, it is not a pleasant experience. I still see myself running from one room to another and trying to think of what I will need to get me through life's necessities for a couple of weeks. I have less than 30 minutes to pack. It's warm here in Florida, and it will be cold up North – how many clothes, not very much room, bring as small an amount as possible. Can you get the picture?

In these stories you'll find I like to make comparisons in life. You'll find a lot of them - living conditions, wages, homes, families, cars, and many more. I just said I didn't know if you had ever received a call or a message like that and felt the fear and confusion I had. You see, I thought I had three more weeks to get ready, not 30 minutes. You may never have to feel what I felt or may never get into this situation, but I can assure you one thing, there is coming a day when Jesus will call you and me home. That, my friend, is a fact, and we may not even have the 30 minutes to get ready. It may be NOW, it's time, let's go. Oh, it would be nice if when the time comes, God will call and say, "Doyle, your bus is leaving in three weeks and you must be ready. Is there any unfinished business you need to see about? Is there any unforgiveness in your heart you need to settle up with? Are there any hurtful words you have spoken that you need to say 'I'm sorry' for? Are there any goodbyes? Anyone to reassure that you love? Anyone to lift up and take care of and encourage on their way? " And then, He might say, "did you tell anyone about me?" And last, He might say, "did you accept my Son, who bled and died on the cross for you, as your savior?"

Yes, wouldn't it be nice of God to give us a few weeks to do those last-minute things, or what if we tried to cram them into the 30 minutes, like I had, to go on the road.

My last thought is, suppose, like so many, He will just say, "take my hand, child, we're leaving right now."

You see, you don't need a toothbrush, comb, or clean underwear on this trip; it's all furnished. If the streets are paved with gold, what will the inside of the rooms be like?

What would you do? You see, that night when I was packing, I must admit thinking these thoughts were the last things that would have crossed my mind. Thanks be to God, in the weeks, months, and years after that night, I had time to rethink it, and it has helped me prepare for that one and glorious trip I'll take.

Maybe just pause at the end of this chapter a bit and chew on these few questions:

1. If God asked, "Did you tell anyone about my Son," how would you answer?
2. If you had a day, or three weeks, or 30 minutes, what would you do?
3. Are you ready?

Lord, don't mind the mule, just load the wagon.

CHAPTER 10
THE NEXT THREE WEEKS

Now, we will get back to Miami and a truckload of shrimp to be delivered to Gloucester, Massachusetts, as fast as we could get there. We had been up all night and were on the road, seems like by noon the next day. We were wrung out when we started. By then, Ben was shifting the gears pretty well and we were finding all the scales to stop at, so we settled in for a long trip. A long, fast trip. We didn't have time to rest. Somewhere in Georgia, Ben says, "Dad, I can't see anymore, we have got to change drivers." Remember, I had not even sat in the driver's seat of a rig. I got up in the sleeper, behind him, and while going the speed limit on Interstate 95, he slid over and I slid down in his place. I could keep it in the right lane and keep the speed up; I just couldn't change gears. He got in the sleeper with his head on the edge and his arm ready. At every set of scales, I would slow down and roll to a stop and wake Ben. When the green light came on, I would mash in the clutch and he would run through the 13 gears and go back to sleep. On-the-road training. I hadn't planned it this way. When you see these big rigs with a 30-foot sign on the side – "Student Driver" – easing around these little towns, think about me trying to learn on I-95, headed for Massachusetts. By now, you are probably smiling, but I tell you it wasn't very funny. By the time we traded back and forth for a little nap and got to New York City, I could find most of the gears. Not good, mind you; I didn't learn as fast as Ben, and was a good bit older. We did learn that any information we needed was on the CB radio, just ask and a trucker was ready to help.

Looks like, to get to Massachusetts on I-95, you go right through New York City. I had taken a couple of trips out West with some of my hunting buddies, riding in a car and a pickup where there was plenty of room for everyone. On the East coast was another story. I had been to the mountains of North Carolina several times, and most of that was on a two-lane road. I definitely couldn't rely on my past experiences. Ben took over when we got to the big cities – too much trouble shifting – and in those days the toll booths in NY were so close together you didn't get through the gears, when you had to stop again. Here we were, coming into Gloucester with our load of shrimp, and where do we go? Got on the radio, it was about midnight when we asked for directions to the address on our load sheet. Someone came right back and called himself Captain Video, who we will never forget. He told us about going into town, what street to get on, and make a sharp left turn on another street and couldn't miss it. We followed his directions to the letter, but when we tried to make that last left turn on the side street, it was just impossible. This is going to be very hard to explain.

Gloucester is something like where I live, St. Augustine, Florida, and trying to turn a tractor and trailer down one of those side streets, it's just out of the question. Of course, that's what the man said, so that's what we were trying to do. Well, Ben ended up with the tractor in an old man's front yard. He comes running out of the house in a long night shirt and a white stocking night cap, saying "back up, you can't do this." I don't know how many of you have ever driven a big rig, but there are times when you can drive your truck in a tight spot, but it will be almost impossible to back it out. (Sounds like some of the lessons in life, doesn't it?)

Anyway, when Ben and I realized we had been had by Captain Video and tried to seesaw our way back, it really got bad. The more we tried, the closer the cab came to the eaves of the house, until his yard must have been a mess. Of course we never saw Captain Video, but I bet he was standing in the crowd laughing at what he had done. Maybe it's a good thing we never saw him, know what I mean? I can still see that stocking cap, made like a Santa Claus cap with a point that falls down on the side of your face. We were glad when it was over, and we found the right address. They were open and backed us in, even though it was midnight. By then we were about dead.

The shrimp were frozen in big boxes and the people came out and told us how and where to stack them. Around 40,000 pounds – could we do it? Lord, where are you? I'm so tired I can't see, and we have to unload a 40-foot trailer. Two of us. We had no choice; it had to be done. When we got through, the only thing we could think of was, we had to catch up on our log book. The law required you to keep account of your time whether driving, resting, or sleeping to the nearest 15 minutes, and don't get behind, you must keep it current. So, being very green at this, we decided to sit in the cab and catch up on the books before we moved. Try to picture this as best you can. We woke up by someone beating on the door telling us to move our truck out of the way. The sun was way up and we were both sitting up in our seats, log book on our lap and pencils in one hand, very fast asleep.

Now for a story about a lady in Pennsylvania that came on the radio as we were asking the directions to the Heinz ketchup warehouse. Of course, we expected a trucker to come on and explain how to get there as usual. But this time, a very polite voice of a lady going in detail from one location to the warehouse was truly a surprise. We took her directions 'cause it had been quite a while since Captain Video in Massachusetts. Later, while we were having the truck loaded, we mentioned it there, and we found out that this was an old lady in a wheelchair on her radio directing truckers around the city. That's just what she did for entertainment or pleasure, or maybe a ministry I'd like to call it. I hoped God blessed her for it.

Here is a short story just for the chuckle. To load your truck with ketchup, you had to back your trailer down this long, narrow alley with buildings on both sides. It seems like it held two trucks with just enough room to clear the mirrors on each side. If you were a greenhorn like me, you would never make it. Ben got good enough to back it down places like that, though. Anyway, I never forgot that long, narrow back-in. Several years later, out on my cookie route, I was at a country convenience store delivering cookies, and as I came out of the store to leave, a semi-truck came up to the front, stopped, cut the front wheels sharp, and with one quick movement put the back of the trailer right to the front door. And, of course, he had to maneuver around the gas pumps. No seesawing back and forth, just one quick try. I don't know why, but I said to the driver as he climbed down from the cab, "Looks to me like you could have been to Heinz Ketchup in Pittsburg." He just kind of froze, pointed his finger at me, and said, "You been there, too?" Just a funny moment in time to remember him pointing his finger and the expression on his face.

I remember going over to the office to get paid. Hadn't shaved or had a bath since we left home. In the rush, I forgot to take a pillow, so the coat I had on looked pretty wrinkled, serving as my pillow. I'm sure we looked a mess. As I sat there waiting for our check, I thought, you know, last weekend I was in church all dressed up (I'm a Sunday school teacher); look at me today. No one would know it now. Lord, where are you?

Afterwards, we got a little rest in the sleeper. I don't think I mentioned it, but this was a single sleeper, so we both had to sleep on our sides for the next two years if we were sleeping at the same time. Not enough room for us to sleep on our back or stomach. If it was warm, we had AC on, or if it was cool, the heater, but no matter what, there was a big diesel engine running a few inches under your bed all the time.

We had our first flat tire heading out, and pulled into a truck stop and woke a man up at two in the morning. The money and time were tight, so we asked him if we took it off and brought it to him, how much would it be to patch the tire. He said $14.50, and we thought that was great. We said we would be back as soon as possible. No problem, he said just to wake him up. We jacked up the trailer, put a long pipe on the huge lug wrench, and one of us had to walk out on the long pipe to get enough leverage to take off the 20 lug nuts. It was a long, tiring job, but we got it off, and woke the man. He patched the tire, and as we were leaving we asked how much it would have cost if he had done it all. He said, "$14.50; it's all the same price, don't charge anything for taking it off." You talk about greenhorns, but we were learning – very slowly.

I need to explain where we were changing the tire. We were on a two-lane road with very small shoulders. There was just enough room to get the truck and trailer off the road. I remember the white line down the side of the road was just past where the tires were. That made the traffic just a few feet or so from where we were standing. No room for a mistake for us or them at two o'clock in the morning. God must be a busy man taking care of people like us.

Some things got better, some stayed the same. Food was one that stayed the same. When we went into any eating place, we opened the menu and whatever was the cheapest offered was what we ate. Once, in the very early days, we were on a two-lane road and saw a fast food place in sight of the road. We were real hungry. Ben turned down the road and realized there was no place to park that much truck or turn it around, so I jumped out, and he said, "I'll be back." I got us a hamburger and some fries and waited and waited. I was really beginning to worry. Finally, here he comes. It was many miles before he found a place to turn it around. We didn't try that again.

It makes me chuckle to think about one day we were getting our truck loaded and had missed breakfast because of the early start. We had driven all night and were about as tired and hungry as you can get. The young man loading the trailer seemed to be very friendly, so I asked him, "If you had been up all night and hadn't had anything to eat since yesterday, where would you go?" In a strange town every day, we needed some help. He didn't even have to think about it. He just said right off, "I'd go to Grandma's house." Good answer from a young man, don't you think?

Soon, we were on the way to pick up a load of frozen mullet for fish food, dolphin, I think, on the coast of Mississippi. The company saw we had two drivers, so we didn't get much time to deliver anything. No stopping, just keep driving. Ben was asleep in the sleeper and I slowed down to ease off the side of a two-lane road. He jumped up and asked what was wrong. I told him when you go to sleep driving, have a nap, wake up and remember all the dream, it's time to pull over and take a nap. So we did.

It took us three weeks to get back to Florida and spend a couple of nights at home before heading out again. To see my wife and family, to sleep in a real bed and eat some home-cooked food again, and go to my church.

Lord, don't mind the mule, just load the wagon.

CHAPTER 11
WHAT WAS IT LIKE?

If you have never been there you might ask, "what was it like?" If you have been there you might have enjoyed it – I don't know. After a few days of this, I knew it wasn't my kind of life, but we were too deep in debt to back out now.

Soon, we were headed back to Garden City, Long Island, with a load of orange juice from Florida. If you were not on time, all kinds of things could happen; wait 'til tomorrow, take it back. They are not kind to late deliveries. Snow and ice everywhere and two Florida crackers trying to get to Long Island and we were running late. When we got to the toll booths in NY, something was going wrong. The air brakes seem to be trying to come on when we slowed down at the toll booths. So we had to keep the RPM's up high and keep the air pressure up in the tanks so the brakes wouldn't stop us. Didn't know what was wrong, but it was serious. We kept the motor screaming at every stop when we paid our toll. We kept watching the gauges and our watches. With everything covered with at least a foot of snow, we were creeping on the street looking for the address, when Ben looked at the gauges, turned the steering wheel and said, "That's as far as we can go."

The brakes locked up and we slid out on an open parking lot in a small shopping area. We'll never make it on time now. As soon as I got my feet on the ground, or ice, that is, I saw this man coming out of a drugstore with an armload of rubbing alcohol bottles and noticed he was headed for a tractor with no trailer. We asked him where the warehouse was, we knew it was close, and it was only about three blocks away. He asked about our problem and we tried to explain as best we could. He smiled and said, you are not used to this cold; that's what this alcohol is for. Just have to keep some in your air lines so the brakes won't freeze up. His trailer was being unloaded as we talked. He said, let's drop your trailer and try to move your tractor enough to get mine under your load and I'll deliver it on time. So we did, and we had plenty of time to go back and put alcohol in our lines, melt the ice, and pick up our trailer. What a blessing!

Now, for the lesson – the driver said he always drops his trailer at that place, comes out and turns to the right, and buys his alcohol at the same store every time. This morning, he turned to the left, and didn't have any idea why he was turning the opposite direction. Of course he said, "Now, I know; don't you know that God takes care of his own?"

That was the first time I had a glimmer of hope; maybe God was out there, after all.

We went back to Gloucester a few weeks later on a Saturday night. On Sunday morning, I got up early, looked in the Yellow Pages, picked out a church in walking distance, and went to a filling station to use the rest room, cleaned up and shaved – kind of a bird bath, you know – and put on the cleanest work clothes I had. I might say they were definitely not very churchy. When I got inside, I'll never forget the feeling of peace that came over me as I eased in the door and sat down. Anyway, away from the worldly noise and diesel engines running, it was so quiet. For a little while it was a feeling of home and belonging and my spirit was at ease.

I stayed for both services, ate breakfast, and even stayed for their meeting on how they were going to serve the tourists in town that coming summer. All morning, I was there, and nobody ever came over to talk or welcome me. I picked up my dishes after I ate and heard one person say, "It's a shame a stranger has to take his own stuff back to the kitchen." They still wouldn't talk to me or welcome me to their church.

After the last service, the priest was shaking everyone's hand on the way out, and I asked for a minute of his time. I told him I was a truck driver from Florida, and I had stayed all morning and listened to them plan on welcoming the tourists this summer, and yet no one would even speak to me, a stranger. He smiled and seemed to know, and asked if I would come back and tell the church my story on Sunday morning. He said his church needed to hear this. I said, "Sure, if I'm ever here again," but it never worked out for me to be there at the right time.

Another lesson – I have been the stranger and you did not invite me in (Matthew 25:43).

Lord, don't mind the mule, just load the wagon.

CHAPTER 12
WHAT SHOULD I LOOK FOR?

I began to realize that the living conditions we were in were so different to what I was used to, and I needed some Christian nourishment of some kind. We were just coming home every two or three weeks for a two- or three-night stay and having to work on the truck, change the oil and tires while we were there.

So, one Sunday morning, going through Beaumont, Texas, I saw a church right beside the road, and told Ben to pull over, we could spare an hour or so. I went in and sat on the back row. It was such a good feeling to be inside, so safe and quiet compared to the garbage I had to listen to on the CB radio. As soon as the service was over, a gentleman reached out his hand and introduced himself, so I did the same. Then he turned and introduced me to the closest one to us and asked if they would take me upstairs for coffee. Boy, this is great, I'm a truck driver, and they are treating me like a guest! At the coffee gathering, here comes the man that I saw first, to find me. My friend, they had a system and a good one. It was not a put-on, because when I started down to the parking lot, one man said, "Why don't you come go home with me and eat with us, we have plenty?" I really wanted to go but explained time was too short. I went back to the truck feeling very uplifted. I guess, because I was a stranger and they took me in, or rather, asked me in. I never did understand why he would ask an out-of-state truck driver, someone he had never heard of, to come go home with him. That day left an impact on me. Someone trusted me, a total stranger, to invite me home with their family. I still can't tell you why.

Making a decision to look for some spiritual nourishment, even as limited as it was, was a good one. There was another place somewhere east of Dallas, where we used to stop, eat and kill a little time before going into the city, and I found a little church just a short distance from the parking lot. So, one Sunday when we were there,

I walked over and was just in time for Sunday school. I was directed by some people to the men's class and was accepted just like someone down the road. It was really fun, just a small group of about eight or ten.

Since we slept at night in the truck at the truck stops, it worked out that I was able to stay over and go several more times to that same little church. One Sunday, at the close of Sunday school, the leader said, "we'll ask Doyle to close in prayer." Here I was, hundreds of miles away from home, being called by my first name and a part of a Sunday school class. This helped a little more. "Seek and ye shall find," it says (Matthew 7:7). There would be times I remember walking across the same parking lot between the truck stop and the church and asking God, "How did I get here? How did all this happen to me? How could I get myself into this mess?" How about you? Have you ever been there, to ask Him why, how, what next? Guess what? He didn't say a thing. I couldn't hear a sound. We just knew we had to keep on and make the best of every day that we could.

I mentioned before the people in the truck stops and the language they used were so different from the environment I was used to. I came out of what I called a "padded Christian community." I was protected from a fall; someone was always there to catch me. The friends were clean, kind, and well mannered. Here, I was thrust into an environment of dog-eat-dog, foul-mouthed people that never looked clean. As a matter of fact, I probably looked the same because we would only take a bath at certain big truck stops. Of course, that was a treat. In most of them, your feet would stick to the tile floor from the soap and dirt off so many truckers, and you have to be sure to put your clothes right in front of the shower curtain, because someone might run off with everything. One night, in Dallas, I walked across the interstate, which was a trauma in itself, to get to a big shopping center I could see. When I got inside the stores, I just wanted to walk up and down the aisles and be around some clean, well-dressed people. I didn't buy a thing, just changed my environment for a short time. It was really refreshing.

Now and then, you would hear a funny story to give you a laugh. Once I was sitting in a small room for the truckers to do their laundry. It was just a place to get in the shade and kill some time, waiting for that phone call for the next load. A young girl in her early 20's was folding her clothes from the dryer. We had seen them before in their old truck painted with a paint brush and named "The Green Lizard." A big burly truck driver sits down, and thinking that he would strike up a conversation with the young lady with no man around, says, "You a truck driver?" Not even looking up, she said, "No, I'm a female interstate commodities relocation engineer." Well, he smiled and was quiet for a minute. Then he wasn't going to give up, so he says, "that your dog?" She says, "Yes." The little fellow was on the floor scratching a little. The trucker says, "He must have fleas." She just said, "No," trying hard not to get into a conversation. He said, "Well, he's scratching." She calmly said, "Do you ever scratch?" He never said another word, finally got up, and left.

I want to add a little about truck drivers in general, especially after the experience with Captain Video, who I'm sure now was not a truck driver. These people do get dirty, they do look bad at times, and so did I. There are so many times you don't have time to bathe, change clothes, and look neat. But they will help another driver in any situation they can. They will go out of their way to help you get to where you are going or lend you a hand at whatever you need. Some are Christians and some are not, just like in our families and neighborhoods. In a trucker's defense, I want you to know they do look out for their own.

Once, we delivered a load and the broker sent us to Circleville, Ohio, to pick up a load of some kind coming to Florida. That was great, going home for a short visit. Only one hitch: we had to wait three days for the load. There was no truck stop in the small town, so it was just sit in the truck in a parking lot for three days. I won't even try to explain; you would have to experience it yourself. Anyway, I go to the Yellow Pages again for a church. There it was, Wednesday night service on Mound Street. When I got to the church it was the right time, but the front door was locked. I go around back to the kitchen and ease in and another door takes me to the church where I could see a service going on. Someone saw me standing there and came over, took me to a seat, helped me with the song book and made sure I was a part. After the service, which was very uplifting, the pastor asked me who I was and where I was from. We talked a bit, and I explained it was tough out there on a Christian. He said, "Let's pray." The entire body gathered around me and laid their hands on me while he prayed. Everyone in that small gathering, which was a body of Christ, was lifting me up. It was a very good feeling. After that, he said, "I live just next door, come home with me." And sitting at the kitchen table, he picked up the phone and said, "What's your home number?" I told him, and he called Marianne and handed me the phone and said, "take your time." What a blessing the Rev. Slack and his people were to me that night. It makes the long waits in the parking lots a little easier. I also was on the church's newsletter mailing list for years after. It was a joy.

We finally came to realize that trying to haul frozen food with the old unit, and then picking up whatever we could to get back wasn't panning out. So we parked our trailer at home and just rented a dry box to haul Nabisco cookies, mostly between Florida, Georgia, and Texas. This kept us "crackers" in the South and out of the snow and ice. My wife had a first cousin in Gulfport, Mississippi, Jim and Cherry Morris. Marianne and Cherry had been close, growing up, and then Cherry would babysit for us when the children were little. So, once in a while on our trips from Texas to Florida, we would have time to stop over and spend a night, eat home-cooked food, go to church, and have fellowship with good Christian people – family, at that. The church accepted us as one of their own and we enjoyed many services and Sunday school lessons with them, too. Once, I remember stopping by to see Jim and Cherry and they were not at home, but the church folks took us in anyway. The preacher took us home with him after church to eat. His wife had been sick and had very little fixed, but when she got the food on the table, my son remembered thinking that there was no way for us and his family to make a meal of this small amount. He still tells of everyone helping their plate, eating all they wanted, and there was still food on the table when we got up. Ben said it was the feeding of the 5,000 right before his eyes.

On one of our overnight stays at Jim and Cherry's home, they had an ice cream social for the church. It was an extra blessing to get in on this. I guess some 30 or 40 people were there. No service, just visiting, talking, and eating ice cream. Good clean fun. As we were being introduced to some people we didn't know, I met a small, dark-complexioned Korean lady who had a very different look about her. I'll try to explain. You could ask her what her name was, where she lived, about her family and whatever, but you didn't need to ask her if she was a Christian. Just look and it was shining all over her. I believe she might have glowed in the dark, but I don't know that for sure. Anyway, as we were talking, she mentioned she used to be a Buddhist and right away, I asked if she would tell me how she became a Christian. She said, "sure," and we sat on the step that was between the dining room and the living room. If you can picture us sitting there with 30 or 40 people, talking and laughing at the same time, but I never heard a sound. It was as if it was all blocked out, to hear her story. She had married an American service man, and after the war came over to the States with him and lived here ever since. She was very happy being a Buddhist and prayed to Buddha every day and was very satisfied with her life. Then a neighbor began to invite her to church. Of course, she would always give her some excuse and try not to hurt her feelings. She said she had no intention of ever going to a Christian church, because she had everything she wanted in her own worship.

Well, her neighbor kept at it until once she asked if she would go to a kid's night at the church for a fun time – seems like she said it was like a Mexican piñata festival – and she told the lady it would be all for fun and Jesus would not be brought up. Well, she thought this would be the perfect time to satisfy her friend and neighbor and not get involved in the "church" part of it and maybe she would leave her alone. I will never forget how she put it. "Well, I went, and they did mention Jesus, and I cried for the next three days without stopping. After that, I have been a Christian ever since." A very simple story, but one I will never forget. She was a powerful witness, not only to her, but to me. The joy seemed to flow from her body. Times like this ice cream social were few and far between, but they gave me strength to keep going.

Lord, don't mind the mule, just load the wagon.

CHAPTER 13
WHAT DID I LEARN IN HOUSTON

It seemed, at times, we spent more time in the 76 truck stops in Houston than any place on the road. Usually, we would unload in Dallas, drive down to Houston, and have to wait, maybe overnight, for a load to leave. It was a time to shower and sleep.

When you drove in the lot, there were acres and acres of semis as close together as you could park, row after row. You go inside for a cup of coffee and whatever is cheap to eat. If you sit at their table and enjoy the AC, you are expected to buy something. There is nowhere else to sit. When you finish, you need to leave so someone else can sit.

I remember bringing my morning reading in with me, to read while I was having coffee. It's a little book put out by radio Bible class called "Daily Bread," and comes every three months. I hadn't missed many mornings in the last 25 or 30 years. Anyway, when the waitress poured my coffee, she asked what I was reading, and I explained. When she came back, she commented again, it must really be good. I could see the need in her face, somehow. When I went back to the truck, I remember saying, "Lord, this is all I have out here," but I couldn't forget the look on her face, so I read the rest of the book and took it back inside and gave it to her. She thanked me and I never saw her again. I do believe she was blessed, and so was I, in giving it.

This truck stop is where I first remember seeing the first video game being played. It was called Pac Man. It was always playing a tune over and over. I can still hear it. It cost $.25 to play, and I got so sick of hearing it in every truck stop, I have never played a video game yet.

Understand now, the truck cab was our home, so temperature was a very important part of our small world comfort. We were in Florida, to Texas, to Massachusetts, never knowing where we would sleep next. If you needed heat or air conditioning, in driving or sleeping, that engine had to be running. If the AC went out, you had to get to the first junk yard and get a used one, stop, put it on, and get back on the road. As I said, money was always in short supply. I can still see a trucker eating about half of a big steak and leaving the rest to be thrown away. I wanted it so bad I could literally taste it, but was too proud to ask him for the rest. It was just times like those that now make my steak taste better than anyone else's around me. We were, as I said, hauling mostly Nabisco cookies from the bakeries to the big warehouses, so usually someone would give us several packages of cookies when we were loading. Of course, when bedtime came and you had a cookie, there was no good cold milk to go with it. One night we were talking about how nice it would be if we had a pint of milk to go with the cookies. We had to spend the night in the bakery parking lot, as we did many times, with no place nearby to buy anything. We got on the CB and asked directions to the nearest store. We wound around the streets in the tractor and finally came to a little convenience store, got our milk, and saw that we were close to the interstate bypass around the city, so we got on that to go back. When we pulled in the parking lot, we realized that we had driven over 45 miles to get the pint of milk for each of us. But, you know what? That's been over 20 years ago, and almost every night, the last thing I do before going to bed is to go to the refrigerator for a little cold milk. Sometimes, it is just a swallow, but I seem to enjoy knowing it's there just for the taking. Sometimes, I think this probably tastes better to me than it does to most folk.

One late afternoon, I was standing up with my Vienna sausages and crackers on someone's flatbed trailer, eating my supper. Another trucker was on the other side, doing the same. He looked up with a dead pan expression and said, "I guess we are eating out tonight, huh?"

Another meal I will never forget was sitting down at the truck stop restaurant, and opening the menu to see what was the cheapest. I mentioned earlier that that was just standard procedure: what kind of food can we get our stomach full on for the cheapest price. But this day, we were really broke. I found a bowl of tomato soup on the list that seemed to be the cheapest food offered. If you got soup, you could have all the saltines you wanted with it. I can still see that bowl of soup – it looked like they poured a little bit of tomato juice in a bowl of warm water, and it tasted like it, too. However, I did soak up enough crackers to get full. I do realize at this point that I'm not the only one who ever went through times like this. Yours might have been worse than the soup. Or better yet, you may have never seen times like this. My point is, I've written it down. So when you eat your next good meal, you can thank God for your blessings. If it helps you to remember a lean time, again you can thank God it's over. My wife is a very good cook and she feeds me well, so many times as I sit down to her good cooking, I don't mention it, but I do think about that bowl of tomato soup quite often.

In those days, I don't know about now, prostitution and drugs were pretty well open. We heard that the cops were afraid to drive in this big truck stop in Houston, and I can believe it, because we seldom saw any kind of law in the lot. It was a very rough environment to stay in, but at the same time, as a trucker, we were safe because they respected one another. They just didn't want any outsiders. With truckers, drugs and prostitutes do not leave much to share the Gospel with.

One night, a young girl, very clean looking, walked by the truck and asked if I needed any company. I told her, "No, thank you," but as she turned to leave, I thought, I'm a thousand miles away from home, why not practice sharing the Gospel with her. We had just left home a couple of days before, and I had some oranges I had picked from my yard. I called to her and asked if she wanted a fresh orange. I'm sure this wasn't the usual response she had been receiving. She said, "Yes, I would," and I tossed her one out the window, telling her that I had just picked it at my home in Palatka, Florida. "Palatka, that's where my baby was born," she replied. Well, I had at least started a conversation; now what? We didn't know each other, and it sounded like she wasn't in Palatka but a short time. Like everyone else, time was money and she was losing money, so she started to leave again. I said, "Wait, I want to know if your mother ever took you to church when you were little." Actually, it was the only line I could come up with that quick. She said, "Why, sure she did, and I go to church every Sunday." Her next line was, "Mister, just because I'm a prostitute, don't you know God loves me, too?" I threw her a little cross I had in my pocket, and wished her well on her way, and she was gone, and I realized I had some more studying to do. I wasn't ready for her statement and didn't have a ready answer for her. So I decided to start making some notes and writing some of this down. It may be interesting some day.

Sometime later in the same truck stop, I had the light on in the cab and was just writing away. Another young girl called and asked if I needed any company and I gave her the same "no, thank you." She paused and asked what I was doing and I said, "well, I'm attempting to write a book." She gave me a big sheepish grin and said, "If you'll let me up in that cab, you'll be able to write another chapter when I leave." I think she was very serious, but so was I, and here I am some twenty years later putting it in a chapter. I guess there is a little humor everywhere.

While we are on the subject of livelihood, I remember another night when two came by and asked if they could get in the cab. My son was off talking to a trucker, and I said to myself, if you are a thousand miles away what have you got to lose? So I said, "yes, both of you come on the driver's side and climb up." They ran around and jumped right up in the driver's seat, and I said, "tell you what, I'll make a deal with you," and shoved a little red New Testament over in front of them, and said, "If you will let us talk about what's in this book first, I'll let you stay all night." Boy, did that throw a damper on their sales pitch. The more outgoing one said, "Mister, what makes it so bad, I know what's in that book. My grandma used to tell me." In a second they were gone. The next night, very late as they were making their rounds and tapping on truck doors, I heard one say, "leave this one alone; there's a preacher in there." Well, there wasn't a preacher in there, but it was a compliment.

I probably never made a difference out there, but I was building up my faith and trying to share it with whoever I had around me.

I have one more lesson of a different nature. As we were leaving Houston late one afternoon, we were closing the doors on the trailer to lock it up, and Ben said, "Dad, we have 90 miles of good road going out of Texas." That meant good sleeping in the cab, for the rest were not all that smooth. He said if I would drive those 90 miles and let him sleep, he would drive on the rest of the night. We had to be in Atlanta early the next day. We were both given out from being up so long, but I said, "sure, I'll try." I stopped just outside of town to fuel up and Ben never stuck his head out, which was unusual. Usually, if we started or stopped, the change would wake him, so I knew he was tired. I got both tanks full, and while I was at it, I saw a tiny Christian fish, maybe two or three inches long, on the door of the next truck fueling up. We sure enjoyed our little conversation – seemed like there weren't too many of us out there. I passed the 90 miles of good road, but hated to wake Ben, and kept on driving.

Later on in the night, I began to wonder if I could go any further. Then, I would say to myself, "well, it says on the sign here, 15 miles to so and so, and I know that's only 15 minutes driving, and I can last that long." When I would get there, I'd pick another sign saying a few miles to exit whatever, and drive to that one. This went on one mile at a time until well after midnight, and my eyes were so scratchy that I couldn't see far. I got on the CB and said, "I've got to have some coffee, I can't go much longer." A trucker found out which truck I was in and said, "Get right behind me and keep talking. I'll show you where some coffee is." I stayed awake talking to him and then he said, "take the next exit." I did, and boy, what good coffee it was! I had several cups and sat around and got awake, crawled back up in the cab and Ben never moved. I eased back out on Interstate 10 and picked another sign to drive to, a few miles at a time. This went on all night, and just as the sun was coming up, Ben stuck his head out of the curtain and asked where in the world we were. We were somewhere in Alabama, just several hours out of Atlanta. We pulled over and traded places, and I passed out, of course. He apologized for the long sleep, but I was so proud to have helped him get the rest.

I really learned a lesson that night when it was quiet and I felt very alone. I knew I couldn't drive far when we left Houston, but I could drive a few miles at a time. Five minutes, 15 minutes, 30 minutes, watching the mile posts beside the road, a mile at a time. I could make it, then another one and the next.

So now, if things are tough, I don't have to face the next week all at once, just an hour at a time, and then a day, and then the next. The Bible says, "Don't worry about tomorrow, for tomorrow will worry about itself," (Matthew 6:34). Each day has enough trouble of its own.

I drove all that night a mile at a time, and I can make life a day at a time, too. Try it, it just might work for you, too.

Did you ever notice about the real lessons in life and when they come along? We were riding along the highway on a beautiful fall afternoon as the sun was setting in the rolling hills of someplace on Interstate 75, on the way to Ohio. You see, I do still have the mental picture and it was pleasant to save in the storage area of my mind. There were no real lessons in it, just a beautiful scene to be captured and enjoyed. The lessons were in the wee hours of the night, when everything was quiet and things weren't all that pleasant. That sometime is when God says, "I have your undivided attention, my child, listen, while I speak."

In Kings 19:11, the Lord told Elijah to go stand on the mountain for the Lord was about to pass by. So he went as he was told and a great, strong wind came, but the

Lord was not in the wind. After the wind, an earthquake, but He was not in the earthquake. After that, a fire, and He was not in the fire. After the fire, a still small voice came, and the Lord spoke to Elijah.

We must train our ears to listen for Him. It may not come over a loudspeaker system; it may be just a whisper of a friend or even a child.

Lord, don't mind the mule, just load the wagon.

CHAPTER 14
WHERE ARE YOU, LORD?

I have mentioned several times asking, "Where are you, Lord – how did I get here, how did I let this happen?" I guess the reason was that I was so uncomfortable out there, I couldn't feel the presence of God. At home with my family and their love, then attending church or church functions, I was in a community of Christians who cared about me and my well-being. He said, "Peter, do you love me?" "Yes, Lord." "Then feed my sheep." (John 21:16-18) I was being fed and encouraged and uplifted by my brothers and sisters in Christ. Out there on the super slab, it's everyone for himself. At the end of a long, hard day, don't be looking to your fellow truckers for compassion. They have had the same kind of day you have had. I have already explained, if I have made myself clear, that any other kind of encouragement or compassion comes with a price tag on it, and thanks be to God, I wasn't seeking that kind. Some trips seem so lonely, because it seemed as if I left my God when we drove away from home and found Him very seldom until we returned again. The question was always there, "Where are you, God, are you here with us in this truck?"

This little story is the most powerful feeling of His presence I experienced in the two years on the road. It took place somewhere in the mountains of Pennsylvania, on a very cold winter night. This was before we started hauling cookies in the South, and I don't remember where we were going, but that doesn't matter. It was in the wee hours of the morning when Ben pulled off the side of the road and woke me from a deep sleep. He said, "Dad, all the trailer lights just went out and we can't drive on until we find out why." I put on my big coat, got my flashlight, and he got his. Our main light was a six-volt battery light that the switch had gone bad on, so we had to twist the wires together to make it work. Of course, we could do this in the dark with no problem. Remember, money was always short. Anyway, after we checked all the main connections between the tractor and the trailer, Ben said, "Well, it has to be a short someplace in the wiring on the trailer." I was still trying to get awake enough to see, when we got under the trailer on the back end. He said, "Someplace on this trailer there is a bare wire touching metal." I wanted to say, "You must be out of your mind," but I didn't. Each little wire was about an inch thick in ice with heavy packs of snow and ice in every crack, packed tight. My next thought was, "and you want me to find a bare wire touching metal when I can hardly find a wire in all this ice." Of course, as I looked up, here come the melting drops down the back of my neck, steadily dripping. Honestly, a needle in a haystack wouldn't have been much different. Ben was a few feet in front of me as we were squatting down searching every wire as best we could. Silently, I decided that now is the time to see if God is out here or not.

I am well aware now, and I was then, of what the Scriptures say about testing God. This night, we were between a rock and a hard place, and we couldn't drive down those very dangerous roads in the icy mountains with no lights. So, I very softly said, "God, if you are out here, please show us where the bare wire is." I have always said that if God answers, you don't have to wonder about it, you usually know for sure. That's just the way God is. Just as soon as I prayed these few words, I saw Ben start moving up to the front of the trailer, crawl out, and stand up, then climb up to the battery box. He called right back, "Here it is, Dad, a pinched wire touching the trailer behind the battery." After my prayer, it was not five minutes later, not two minutes later, but right then, as I watched him never stop moving until he saw the problem.

Then I knew God was there with us and had been all along. I just couldn't see or feel Him. From then on it was still tough, but I knew I wasn't alone. In minutes, he had the wire fixed, and we were on the road again. So now, I still ask at times, "God, where are you," but I have the past experience to go on. "Lord, if you were with us in the late hours of a dark, icy night in the mountains of Pennsylvania, I know you are with me now."

Now that I could deal with life a little better, maybe I was being prepared for what was to come. One day we stopped at a rest station, seems like it was in South Carolina, and Ben called home. Most of our communications with home in the last two years had been by phone. When he came back, he climbed up in the cab and very soberly said, "Well, Dad, it's either my marriage or this truck." I didn't even have to think about my answer. "No truck is worth your marriage. Let's go home." Very soon, we made our arrangements to quit driving. The truck and trailer still weren't paid for, so we had to give it back to its owners. Ben got another job in an auto repair shop, and I got a job delivering cookies to the local stores. I was used to hauling a 40-foot trailer full of cookies, and here I was selling packages half dozen and dozen at a time. What a change, but that was all well and good. We were back with our families and had healthy marriages.

What can I say that I learned in this two-year stay on the road? As I look back and ask myself this question, I guess there were many lessons for my good. Things like a good bed to sleep in at night – and it's not moving. A refrigerator close by at all times and always a gallon of good, cold milk in it for that little drink at bedtime. A hot shower anytime I want one, and my feet don't stick to the floor. It's nice not to have to fill up at meal time on the cheapest food offered. We are blessed to eat very well at our home. My wife is the best cook a man could dream of. To be in church every Sunday and worship with family and friends. In other words, I enjoy my life more now because of what I didn't have before. Do you take life for granted and think that it will always be like this? When it's meal time, I can eat; when it's bedtime, I can sleep; when it's cold, I can get warm; and when it's hot, I can cool off. God has blessed me so much.

I have four children and 10 grandchildren now to bring me joy, and the farthest one away is only 50 miles.

On a more serious note, I have a loving wife who has stood by me through all the hard times, who still loves me for who I am. I think I appreciate her much more now because of the time when we had only the pay phone. Thank you, Lord, for Marianne.

The last lesson I feel is a very important one. It's one I probably couldn't learn out of a text book. When you are a thousand miles away from home and want to learn to share the Gospel with someone, especially if you don't know much about how to do it, you practice on whoever is available. This is probably the most important lesson I learned: not only how to, but how not to be afraid of trying.

I'll probably be referring to a lot more lessons or stories throughout the rest of the book, because as I have said, those two years are where the writing idea came from.

So now, I can say to you all, I highly recommend the course I took, but not the school I attended.

Lord, don't mind the mule, just load the wagon.

CHAPTER 15
BACK HOME

Well, it was so good to be back home again – sounds like a John Denver song, doesn't it? Back home with my family, feet under my table, and sleeping in my bed every night. Able to go to church every Sunday. How is the money situation? About like it was when I left to go on the road, but it seems like we could deal with it better at home. That big green monster of a truck was sitting in the yard for a while as we were trying to sell it and reclaim a few thousand of what we were about to lose, but nobody wanted a used semi. Every morning when I looked out the kitchen window at it sitting there, it was like peeking under a bandage looking at a cancer on your arm, if that makes any sense. It has been bad news dealing with it for two years, and it seems like it just won't go away. Finally, we just gave it back to the owners and bit the bullet. I was glad to have it out of the yard.

Now, I'm off on the cookie truck, which was just a GMC step van with three-speed transmission. No problems.

Now it's time for my first real lesson in humility.

The lesson came on the floor of a Publix grocery store. Remember now, we were the ones that were having a real adventure, driving the big rig, out with the big boys, and seeing the country first hand, sleeping in a different state every night. Well, now that was gone, and I was on my knees, stocking cookies on the bottom shelf, when an old friend walked by, looked down, and said, "What in the hell are you doing down there." Then I would have to explain that it didn't work out. Talk about eating crow – I had to explain to lots of my old friends what I was doing. I tried to smile when I was telling the same story, but it was hard at times. Lord, it's hard to be humble.

I was invited to speak at a couple of churches close by, and they were glad to see me back and wanted to hear my story. It wasn't as scary to talk as before; it seems a lot of the fear left me on the road.

I hadn't really thought about it before, but yesterday, I heard a preacher on the radio saying that many times after a spiritual experience, there comes a test of some kind. Then I thought about Jesus being baptized by John in the Jordan River and the Spirit descending on him. What could be more perfect than that – God sending his Spirit down on his son so powerful that it was even visible as a dove, it says in Luke 3:22. Then what happened? He was led by the Spirit into the wilderness for 40 days to be tempted by the devil.

As I was writing the last paragraph, I realized that years ago when I finally got my spiritual feet on the ground and could feel the Spirit in my life for the first time, what happened? I seemed to be led in the wilderness for the next two years - tempted by Satan with everything in his book. Please don't get me wrong. I can never compare my life to Christ, I can only say as the speaker on the radio said, that after a good experience comes a test. Yes, maybe it was. Then, last night at church, a friend told us that after the Spirit comes, then will come proof, and after the proof, comes the commission to do His work. She was saying that after the Spirit coming at Pentecost, Jesus gave them proof, "Here, see the nail prints in my hand, and put your hand in my side and feel where the spear went in." He wanted his disciples to know for sure and have no doubt who they were following.

So now, I believed that I had been exposed to his Spirit and had asked if He was with us on the road, which after the lights went out, I knew He was. It was sort of the first lesson, in proof. Then came a period of time when I began to realize that Christ was alive, was real, was with me, and His power was here to be used by folks like you and me.

One of the first miracles of prayer was to take place with my mom. It was our yearly visit for our Bishop, Frank Cerveny, to our church. This was always a joyous Sunday. He is such a good preacher and knows just how to lift your spirits personally. He can also create enthusiasm for a small church to move forward. If I recall correctly, we had a big breakfast, then church, because he and Emmy, his wife, had to go to St. Marks in Palatka for their visitation. He had known my mom, and he asked right off where she was. We told him she hated to miss the visit, but she was in bed with a bad back. Here I need to explain what I mean by a bad back. Each time she hurt her back, it always got worse. So this time, she was in the bed and we were taking her meals to her. We had been to her doctors and made several trips to the emergency room because of the very severe pain. Also, I had a close friend, David Harrell, in our church who was a pharmacist and owned his own drug store. I had called him as a last resort to see if he would give Mom any stronger pain medicine. He assured me that the last pills were as strong as her body could stand and it would be very dangerous to increase it.

So this Sunday, we left her in bed and dashed over to the church to help with breakfast and hear our bishop preach, clean up the dishes, and hurry back home.

As he was leaving to go to St. Marks for a later service, he said, "We are going by to see Helen on the way." Of course, I thanked them because Mama loved them just as we did and she only got to see them several times a year, at the most.

Anyway, we helped clean up after church and rushed back home to care for her, and to our surprise, she was up in the kitchen cooking. They had come in, gotten on opposite sides of the bed, and prayed for the healing of her back. Then they rushed on to Palatka. It was a very simple prayer, and God answered it. She cooked our supper that day and never was down with her back again. This was probably sometime in the 1980's, and she died in December, 2010. In February, she would have been 104 years old.

So when God does the healing, there is no mistake who gets the glory.

After I witnessed this answer to prayer, I thought, if it worked for Bishop and Emmy, why not try it myself? I want to share a few of these stories with you.

One Sunday afternoon, I was helping at a church camp and the weekend was over. Everyone was packing up to go home. A lady came and asked if I could look at her car, because it wouldn't start. There are a lot of things I am not, and an auto mechanic is one of them. Anyway, I ran out back and took a quick look, and seeing it was a Honda, I knew I was lost for sure. A Ford or a Chevy, maybe if the problem was very obvious, I might see it. I quickly turned the key, looked under the hood for a wire that might be off, and then looked around, and all the men who might have been of some help were gone. What next? This car wouldn't even make a sound. I remember sitting down in the driver's seat, gripping the steering wheel, and saying, "Lord, I don't have any idea what to do with this lady's car; will You please help me get it started?" Once more, I turned the key, and it started at a touch. Thank you, Lord, You are so good.

I went back inside and told her the story, and I did leave it running. I didn't want to push my blessing too far! I advised her not to shut it off until she was in a more populated place than the church camp. She thanked me and I thanked God, because actually, I only turned the key. Off she went, and her Honda was sounding as good as new. We lived a long way apart, but I would see her from time to time at church functions, and of course, ask about her car. As well as I can remember, she kept the car about two more years and it never failed her again. She never even had it checked out. I called and He answered – simple as that.

Now as you might know, having this little task under my belt, we might just try that again. Christ is real; He does hear our prayers. Can't you just see Jonah wading out in knee-deep water and rinsing off a bit after being in the belly of the great fish and saying, "Why didn't I pray a little sooner, or better yet, why didn't I just go to Nineveh like God asked and not head for Tarshish which was many miles in the other direction?" Speaking about getting out of Dodge, he was serious. I fish a lot, and I have cleaned many a fish in my time, and one of the smelliest things on earth is a fish's belly – even a fresh fish and even a little one. So, one big enough to swallow a man – my bet is that it must have been a stinking place to be.

So, here he is doing a bit of laundry by the seashore and probably hoping no one would pass by and ask him what was going on. How would you answer that? "Jonah, what are you doing, and what in the world is that smell? How on earth did you get so messy?" He might have said, "Well, you may not believe this, but on the way to Tarshish, some guys threw me out of a boat, and a big fish swallowed me and then spit me up here on the shore. So, I'm trying to clean up a bit before I get back on the road." Now, I want you to realize, I have put some conversation in this Bible story for the mere purpose to raise a chuckle. The bottom line is, Jonah had gotten himself in a very inconvenient place to call for someone to help him.

Getting back to my story, I - like Jonah - had learned that when God says, "If you need me, just call," He's serious. He means just that: call me.

The next story finds me at a meeting at my friend Dick Wikerson's home in Jacksonville Beach. There were probably about 30 of us men there meeting in small groups. At a short break, a close friend from Jacksonville came to me and asked if I could open his Cadillac, as he had locked his keys in his car. He said, "I have another set, but it sure is going to be embarrassing if I have to call my wife from across town to bring them to me. You understand?" No, problem; I understood. First break we had I ran out with a coat hanger to give it a try. Well, it wasn't like my old pickup, this car had electric locks. This is sort of out of my league. I tried everything, and nothing worked. I sure hated to fail because I could see in his face that he sure didn't want to call his wife. As I was praying, "What now?" I suddenly reached over to the back door, pulled the handle, and it came right open. Man, is this strange, or what? I reached over in front, picked up his keys, opened the front door, and went back inside to find him. He was still in a small group of men, so I just threw him the keys and went on. Boy, you should have seen his face light up as he picked them up.

After that, I knew that somehow God had a lesson in this for me other than getting the keys. In the next little while, that still small voice seemed to say, "The next time you come up with a problem you can't seem to solve by the method you are using or the seemingly right approach you are using, then use another method or entirely different approach, for it just might work." God teaches many lessons in many different ways, but we must be obedient enough to listen.

The following week, I went to a locksmith and a security system place in St. Augustine. I knew the owner, and I told him I had opened the back door of the Cadillac and the front doors were still locked. He said he believed me, but it should be impossible, because it just isn't built that way. That was good enough for me. With God, all things are possible.

My friend did the same thing. He went to a Cadillac dealership and they had the same story: It just doesn't work that way.

I have yet another story about God's power. One afternoon, Bill Ticknor and I rode over to Matanzas Inlet to try for a red bass. He loved to fish in the surf as much as I did. I do need to explain who Bill is before we get started on our fishing trip. He and his wife, Shirley, lived just a few doors from us in Grandview on the river in East Palatka. They had five children at that time – Laura, Bill Jr., Joyce, Kathy, and Stephen; later they moved to River Groves, several miles away, and Julie and Rachel were born there. Our children were so close, playing together, and at meal time you had to look close to see who belonged to who. Bill was my very best friend and Shirley was Marianne's. Just two big happy families.

So, as you see, now and then Bill and I needed to ease over to the beach, just the two of us, to enjoy each other and fish a little.

This particular afternoon, the tide was very high and rushing out of the inlet, and we were on the south side where the inlet spills into the ocean. We were standing there in knee-deep water with our lines out in the swift current. Then a man came along followed by two little boys playing in the water. The little ones stepped off into the dropoff and were being swept out by the water. The dad saw this and started after them. The smallest kept going, and the older, maybe about seven, started swimming with all his might, and finally made it back to shore. The dad reached the youngest one and got his feet on the bottom across the slue from us. He held the child up, but he was in neck-deep water so swift he could hardly stay there. We could tell that if he even moved, he would be swept out with the swift current.

Now all this happened in just a few seconds. We were reeling in our lines to decide what to do. I was never a good swimmer, but Bill was; he just handed me his pole and said, "I'm going." By then, some people were gathering around us, and I sent some little boys to get some surfers a short distance away so we could get a surfboard to them. Bill was tall and strong, so when he got his feet on the sand by the dad and the young boy, they had some support in the raging surf. In just minutes, here came the surfers with their board. Two young men and one board went out to them. As they were going out, I was twisting my hook off the wire leader on my fifty-pound test fishing line. I left the eight-ounce fishing lead on the line so I could throw it to Bill. When the boys reached them, they got the little fellow on the surfboard, and the dad, Bill, and the two surfers held on. I had to cast a couple of times before Bill caught my line. It was not a life-and-death situation then, but if they went on out, it would take a long time getting back. I started reeling in the line very slowly, and I realized I had never had nearly this much pull on my old surf rod. A fifty-pound test line with four men, a child, and a surfboard against the very strong current. We were gaining a little at a time until a wave would hit them and I would have to give them a little line, knowing it would break if I didn't.

A big crowd had gathered by this time to watch. Well, the line did hold together, and inch by inch they crossed the swift water until they got their feet on the sand. I remember the dad tried to thank us, but he could hardly talk. All was well. Bill turned to me and said, "I think we need to go home; that's about all the excitement we need for today." I agreed, and we left.

All this happened as soon as we got there, so we didn't get to fish at all. The next day, Bill says, "Let's go back and try it again." Of course, I was ready, so off we went still talking about saving the dad and son the day before. We walked down to the same spot at the inlet to fish. Bill was already rigged from the day before, and all I had to do was put a hook on the same wire leader that was still on my line. After doing this and baiting it with a chunk of mullet, I laid the bait and sinker on the sand, drew back ready for that long cast to deep water. Would you believe that at that fast whip of the eleven-foot fiberglass rod and the same eight-ounce sinker from the day before, I heard a crack and my line snapped. The fast whip of the rod had caused the eight-ounce lead to break the fifty-pound test line. Yes, the same line that had pulled in 5 people and a surfboard against the outgoing tide on it the day before.

I'll let you be the judge. Of all places that God can show you His power, can it be concentrated in a fifty-pound test fishing line? I believe it can, and I believe he allowed it to break with just the eight-ounce lead sinker the next day to prove it.

Christ is real, He is here, and He does answer prayers. So, it's time old Doyle started using it.

I was still in the cookie truck, and to be very honest, I wasn't doing very well. I was barely making a living and I was working for a man that I didn't know God made people like him. He was just impossible to please, and it seemed that every way I turned was wrong to him. When he would visit my area, I would get almost sick just to see him coming. Maybe God put him in my life so I would treat people around me better and never be like him. I'm sure glad that part of my life is over. Praise God.

One day, after a long route around the county, I stopped by the Goodyear store where my son, Ben, had gone to work after our return. Of course, it was just to say "hi" and check on him. As soon as I got in the shop, he started telling me about this man's car air conditioner with a leak that had everybody in the shop stumped. They had spent so much time on hunting the leak, there was no way to charge the man this much money. They had even called other shops around the state to get advice on what they might try. Nothing had worked. It seems like it had gone on two or three days. Well, here comes old Dad in, looks over in the front at the AC unit and says, "Have you prayed about it?" Guess how that went over? I can tell you that the store manager didn't laugh out loud. He did say, "I'll tell you what. If you think you can pray and get an answer as to how to fix this man's car, I'll be in your church next Sunday morning." When he said that, I knew for sure he was going to lose. In a few minutes, I wished them well, got in the truck and left. As I was driving off, I said, "Lord, here's your chance. They don't believe prayer works like I do. Just show them where the Freon leak is in the AC." I smiled to myself, because somehow I knew what was going to happen. A day or two after that, I got into town kinda late and stopped by my son's house, and he was already home from work. The first thing he said as I was getting out of the truck was, "Dad, you know what happened right after you drove off from the shop?" I smiled and said, "Yes, I can guess." Sure enough, they found a small hairline crack in a nut on a Freon line they had been missing. It was not even a surprise to me this time; I just knew. Of course, I went by a few days later to draw the manager a little map to our country church, but he wasn't very interested and really didn't want to carry on much conversation. But that's OK, my faith was strengthened and my belief made stronger.

Boy, now as you can see, my life has had another change. I'm back home with my family, in contact with my Christian community, and beginning to witness some of God's power at work in answered prayers.

Lord, don't mind the mule, just load the wagon.

CHAPTER 16
MY AUTOGRAPH BOOK

When I was a small child in grammar school, autograph books were very popular among lots of children. If you can remember those, you have already eased yourself in a certain time slot. Of course, if you can't, we will put you in another age. For a little humor, if you simply don't remember any of this kind of stuff, we will put you in another category that has to do with memory, which is another subject altogether, and I'm not going there at all. That would be another chapter, wouldn't it? Know what I mean?

So anyway, I bought me one of these little books, hard back, about four by six inches. We would cart them around and get our family, friends, and whoever to write us a cute little poem or saying in it and sign their name. All good, clean fun. You would get things from your aunt or cousin like "roses are red and violets are blue, sugar is sweet and so are you." Then some of mine were a little different, like "roses are red and violets are blue, my feet stink and so do you." Just collecting them was fun, whether it was serious or for a laugh.

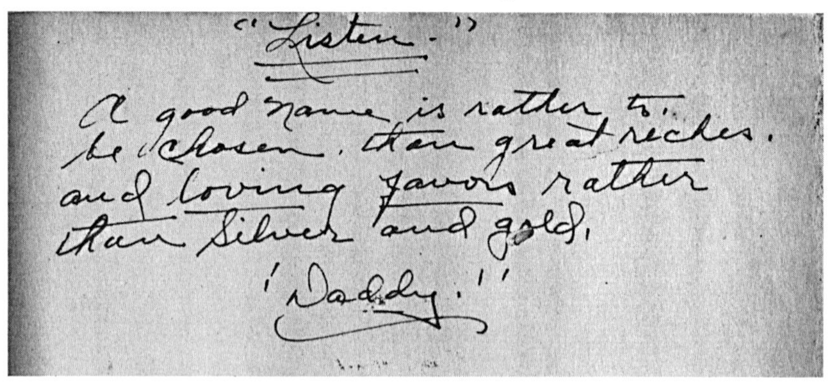

My Autograph Book

Then I asked my dad to write me something. I must admit to you it took me many years to understand why of all the funny little sayings or poems he could have written in my book, he would pick something out of the Bible. It just didn't seem to fit the occasion. That was then and this is now. As I pick up that little weather-worn book now and then, that spent many years in the attic of our home on the river, it has taken on an entirely new meaning. The rats moved in at one time to make a winter home, so there isn't much left of the autograph book now. What the rats left, the termites tried to finish. Praise God, most of the page he wrote on is still there and readable. It's from Proverbs 22:1. "A good name is rather to be chosen than great riches, and loving favor rather than silver and gold." And isn't it strange that of all the pages that are left, this is the only one I can remember. Of course, as I mentioned, without telling him, why would he write this? Yes, he knew, he knew what I would need long after the autograph book craze was over and the fun of the collections was past, what I would need to carry with me into adulthood. That little piece of paper with holes all through it has helped guide and form my life as a man, a Christian man.

I have failed so many times, but just after I did, I knew I had failed because of what those few lines said in Proverbs. I've spent a lot of my life trying to work on my name, and also a lot of time in prayer when I failed to do it.

Here's another story or two about names or what's in a name. I didn't tell you how I got out of the cookie business. As I said before, I was hardly making a living at it when I was called to attend a meeting in Lake City, some 75 miles away. I just couldn't imagine what was so important. Well, after a lot of "very non-important" talk, the company announced it had decided to sell us our route. It would be like owning the franchise. Up to that point, all I had to furnish was the truck and gas. Now, each route was worth a different amount according to how big or small the sales were. They had a short formula to set the price. Each district supervisor would then come around to help you decide on how to set up payments for it. I well remember mine coming to me and saying, "Your route is worth $17,000; we need to work out a plan. Well, I know I'm not the sharpest knife in the drawer, but I knew what my answer would be. I said, "I wouldn't give you ten cents for this route, much less $17,000." In the near future, they came to pick up the keys for the storage shed where I kept the supply for the next week. They sold the route to a good man who had been my neighbor as a child. Of course, the company would not let me know who it was until after he had signed all the papers. It was too late then for him to back out.

That left me doing whatever I could for the next two years to make a dollar. My youngest, Keith, was still at home, so we were mowing a few yards, and my friend, Barry Mahr, had a sand blasting business and was able to use me part time now and then. He got a call from St. Joseph's Academy in St. Augustine to blast off some graffiti on their outside wall. Let me explain that the sand blast would tear up your clothes so bad, and we were usually blasting and painting farm equipment. The spray gun and paint would take care of the rest. Lots of times, you just threw the old clothes away and put on something else that was old and ragged. We started this job, and I had on the worst clothes you could imagine. A fine man was there working on the grounds, and he said that their maintenance man had just quit and he was helping them out until they could hire someone. Well, as soon as I could find the new principal, I asked him about the job. It didn't take him but a minute to say they had already hired a man. As I walked away, I took a good look at myself and my general appearance, and I didn't blame him a bit. I wouldn't have hired me, either. Right after work, I rushed home, took a shower, put on some nice clothes, and came back. He was still there. I asked if I could have a minute of his time. He said, "Sure, come in and sit down." I told him I needed a job, but first I wanted to tell him what kind of person I was. Now, I must be honest, I don't have any idea what I said other than it was the truth. I just wanted him to know there was something more than the ragged person he talked to earlier. I did most of the talking, and only remember the one question he had at the last, "Can you start in the morning?" It was good news for me and my wife.

This was another very important lesson I was learning after so many years ago of my dad writing in my autograph book, "Proverbs 22:1, a good name is rather to be chosen than great riches, and loving favor rather than silver and gold." I was being hired on my name and character rather than on my appearance. It was to be my last job before my retirement, and he became my close friend. Sometimes in life there come times when you must convince a person who you are and what you stand for when there is no one else around to speak up for you.

I would like to mention one more time when this became necessary. It was on a late Wednesday afternoon, and for some reason Marianne had gone on to church and I was to come on as soon as I could. I remember rushing the last few miles through the farm land, trying to get there on time. On the right side of the road was a young lady or girl, maybe 18 or 20 years old, with her thumb up to catch a ride towards my church. I stopped, she got in, and she said she wanted to get to a main highway. I explained to her that in the direction of our church there was no highway, only a dead end. All I could tell was that she was very upset. I then explained that we were only about two miles from church. She tried as best as she could to tell me she wanted to get to a highway so she could catch a ride home, some 30 or 40 miles away. I knew something bad must have happened, and she finally told me that she had just been raped two times by two men who had carried her from St. Augustine Beach. In those two miles, I had to convince her of what kind of person I was and that I would not hurt her in any way. But I needed to tell my wife that I would be much later getting to church. When we left the church, all she wanted to do was get home and take a bath. Again, it took some talking on the way to the main road for her to trust me and believe that I wanted to help her. She said that in no way was she going to the law. Again, I had to convince her of my character and also tell her of my close friend in the sheriff's department. I didn't have long or much to stand on, but after explaining to her that if we didn't try, those two young men would do the same to someone else, finally she said yes, and we went to the sheriff's office and called my friend. They took her in and got a lady on staff to tend to her needs and I left. I never heard a word about the story after that.

The lesson for me was that sometimes you have to convince someone who you are, that you can be trusted, and you may have only a few minutes to do it in.

Lord, don't mind the mule, just load the wagon.

CHAPTER 17
WHEN DOES CHRIST BECOME REAL?

That is a very big question for me, for you, and for the world. On paper, I can tell already it's going to be hard to explain, but if you were sitting here, it probably wouldn't be any easier. Might as well be honest, don't you think? I hope you have read the children's story of the Velveteen Rabbit. If you haven't, please do before you get any older; it is priceless. There is a place in the story where the child's velveteen rabbit asks the old toy skin horse in the bedroom, "When do you become real?" The old skin horse that's been around for a long time tries to explain to the new toy, "Well, it's something that happens when you're loved. It's hard to explain to a new rabbit. It's just something that happens." "Well, does it hurt?" asks the rabbit. "Sometimes," answers the skin horse.

You can see for yourself how long I put this off in this book, but I feel it must be done. When does Christ become real in your life? We know, and I pray that you do know for sure, that He is real, but when is He real in your own life?

Back in the storybook, the skin horse tells the rabbit, "By the time you become real, most of your hair has been rubbed off, and most of your tail has been pulled out," giving him the impression that he may not look so great when he does become real.

How true it is in life. For many of us, by the time Christ becomes real to us, we have weathered many a storm, maybe a shipwreck or two, and crossed several deserts, so we may not appear to be the model Christian as far as looks go.

In the family environment I was raised in, I had no problem believing in God, in Jesus his son, and as I matured, his Holy Spirit.

The Primitive Baptist churches, seems to me, were always out in the woods. I went with my family regularly, until I started dating my wife, and then I started attending the Episcopal Church with her. As a child, I remember, the Primitive Baptist churches were very simple churches, usually. There was no paint, there were pine benches for pews, and no screens, just pushup windows. Sometimes the local funeral home would furnish cardboard fans with thin wooden handles for summer, and there was usually a wood stove in the middle of the church for heat in the winter. The one my dad preached at was this sort of church, with a very sandy two-rut road leading to it. In dry times you had to be very careful not to slow down in the white sand or you were there to stay. Most of the preaching was directed to mature Christian adults and very little for the children. We children were just supposed to sit there and be quiet. There was no music, no notes in the song books. You sang the tunes you learned by going with your folks.

This little story is probably just for me. It may not benefit you in any way. I do feel I need to put it down on paper.

The Primitive Baptist Church I was brought up in was very different as to the way the mainline churches are today. These Christians believed in the same God, the same Jesus, and the same Holy Spirit as we worship today. This story has to do with how one becomes a preacher in the church. In most churches today, after you feel God's calling to preach his word, you must be approved by a committee of some sort to judge if you are sincere in this endeavor. If you are, then you spend a number of years in a school of the church's choosing to learn about Bible history and the many subjects of teaching God's people. As I came from a family of Primitive Baptist preachers – father, grandfather, great-grandfather, great-great grandfather, and many uncles – I was well aware and watched closely how they were chosen. As I can recall from a small child, someone in the church saw something in a man that was worthy of encouragement. Usually, after this encouragement, he was invited by the preacher in charge of his church to speak at a church service. This could go on for a long time – months and months, I don't really remember. If it didn't work out as to his ability to preach God's word, he just wouldn't be asked to speak anymore. Then, much later, if his preaching ability seemed to be pleasing to the people and he agreed to go farther with it, the elders in the church would start making arrangements for him to be ordained as a minister in the church. I cannot tell you what all this involved except I do know that at the last day it took a group of ordained preachers and the laying on of hands.

Well, what I'm getting around to is if they ask old Doyle someday to say something in church, what was I going to do? This was a big question in a young boy about to be a teenager. I knew I would not volunteer, but because of who I was and the Moody family history, there was a good chance that the time would come someday. My grandfather, William Moody, was well known for his preaching and especially for helping settle trouble in small churches. He was never called anything but "Coon Moody," his nickname, and his sister was called "Poss." I have no idea where this came from. Coon Moody the preacher and to all his nieces and nephews it was Uncle Coon and Aunt Poss.

Now getting back to my story of a plan, do I refuse to get up and speak or do I plan on a story to tell someday in the distant future. I decided maybe I'd just get me a story and tuck it away in the back of my mind and leave it there, just in case I needed it.

In 1947, my dad bought a new Plymouth. Whenever he bought a new car, the first thing we had to do was ride over to the "scrub," as we called it, or the Ocala National Forest, for a ride. We had a camp at Salt Springs where we hunted in the fall and fished in the summer. State Road 19 was not built in those days, so we had to go from Palatka to Johnson, turn south, go through Bay Lake, where we went to church, and to Fort McCoy. Then we had to turn back east, cross the Ocklawaha River at Eureka, and go on to Salt Springs. Quite a trip. So, on this trip, we left late in the afternoon. On the way to the camp and just before we got to Eureka, the lights went out on our brand new car. I remember I was driving – I was only 13 at the time, and yes, I did start young. I eased off the side of the road.

It was a very dark night, but we could see the lights at the store in Eureka probably a half a mile away or maybe a little more. Dad said, "Do you think you can get us to the store where the light is on and maybe we can find our trouble?"

A thirteen-year-old boy thinks he can do almost anything, so I said, "Oh, yes. I can do that." I well remember driving very slow and having to keep my eyes glued on that light at the store. There were no houses or cars on the road, just that dim little light far down the road. I remember not even being able to see the pavement on the road. No looking from side to side, just not being able to take my eyes off that dim light, and driving very slowly toward it. We finally made it and never hit a thing. It was a very scary little trip.

We got out and checked everything we could think of and finally found a blown fuse. Of course, we had no fuses, but Daddy knew if we had something to wrap the fuse in to make contact, we might get the lights to work. Well, here again it "just so happened" that before leaving the grocery store in Palatka I grabbed a Nestle's Crunch chocolate candy bar. And you might remember, they were wrapped in a thin aluminum foil. I got out my candy bar, and Dad said he believed that foil would work. We wrapped the fuse, snapped it in, and we had lights.

In 1947 at 13 years old, I had my story. As long as I held my eyes on that light, I could go to my destination without wandering off the road. So it is in life: if we keep our eyes on Jesus, the light of the world, we can stay on the road. It would be a very short and simple story if I ever needed it. Well, I was never called on, I never needed it, I've never used it, I've never told it, and this is the first time I've ever written it down. From 1947 to 2011 is a long time to carry a short, simple story, but isn't that the Gospel story – short and very simple.

I need to add here that I have spoken in church at many occasions. I taught Sunday school for at least 20 or 25 years, and had our Wednesday night services for around two and one-half years. There were times at our small church when on a Sunday now and then I would fill in for our priest. So you can guess how many stories I have had to use in the past 30 years. Again, for some unbeknownst reason, I just never used this one.

Now for a story my grandpa told me – as told to him by another old timer before his time. The preacher was preaching and a man in the congregation was sitting by an open window, when an old Indian walked up on the outside. He just stood there for a short time, and then (now this is in the days when Seminole Indians still lived and roamed the woods here in Florida) he turned to the man sitting right inside and said, "That man," (meaning the preacher), "has been out to my old black stump." Grandpa probably told me this about seventy years ago, when I was a young boy. It has been an inspiration to me ever since. The same God, through his Holy Spirit, who was revealing himself to some of his children through the preacher, had revealed himself at an old black stump, somewhere out in the woods, to this Indian. It was his "altar," if you will.

Stop and pause for a moment, and in your mind's eye, picture an old Indian in his rough native dress, probably barefoot, kneeling at an old black stump. Maybe it was on some sand hill far back in the woods. Maybe there was a big pine stump that never completely burned to the ground when lightning hit it. Picture this Indian kneeling there in silence and reverence, to his Lord and Maker.

You see, God doesn't need a high gloss of six coats of varnish on an oak altar or padded cushions to kneel on or fancy red carpet to walk up to it. He can speak to his children just as we do, even when they are kneeling in the dirt in front of a stump.

People and cultures change; God doesn't change. He will, at times, give us the ability to recognize the evidence of the Holy Spirit in others, that is, if we have received it by something in common. Stories like this, if we don't write them down, are lost. This is one of the biggest desires of this venture, so you might read about the Indian and tell your children and they might tell their children. You see, after going to the small Primitive Baptist churches all my life, I had nothing to compare it with. We went to our church once a month and would visit other churches in the area on the other Sundays, hear other preachers, and meet other Christians. We had dinner on the grounds every Sunday; today, they call it "covered dish." I still remember after I had finished my plate of all my favorites, I'd go back for a little more chicken and rice and banana pudding, and I would eat this together. I know that's a little off the subject, but I want you to know where I'm coming from. In the winter, one of my cousins would quietly get up while my dad was still preaching, and put a pot of coffee on the wood heater so it would be made when church was over. It was just a big enamel pot of water and the coffee grounds were put in it to boil – very simple coffee making. Seems like she knew about how much longer it would be. Was Christ becoming real back then? Yes, very slowly. He was making a way into my heart. Even at times as a child, when I was so bored, I was storing up what was being said and sung for years later. Sometimes, when I was bored, I would find a small round dot of sunlight on the floor coming through the split shingle roof and put my shoe there just to see how long it took for the sun spot to move off my shoe. My, haven't times changed!

What I'm getting around to is my first trip with Marianne to the Episcopal Cathedral in Jacksonville. It was the biggest church I had ever seen in my life. There was carpet on the floor, cushions on the pews, lots of candles on the altar, and when the organist hit the first chords on that huge organ, I actually wanted to crawl under the seat. Talk about change – that, my friend, was change for old Doyle.

You see, it took things like this to make me understand the old black stump story. Once I could understand that the same Spirit was in that big fancy church that was in the little unpainted church in the woods at Bay Lake, Florida, then I knew what the old Indian meant. We did have something in common.

When does Christ become real? I believe He becomes real in your life and mine when He knows we are ready to receive Him. I went through a span in my life where one day just led to the next, and life seemed to be a real struggle. I guess things would make me happy at times, but deep down there was no real joy. It was gone and I didn't know how to get it back. You may have even been there yourself. Or you may be headed in that direction. Now, I don't want to discourage you, but mine lasted for five years. I tried every way possible to cover it up and hide it as best I could. Nonetheless, it was very real. My wife had received something in her spiritual life that I did not have. I didn't know what it was, how to get it, or even for sure if I wanted it. There were times when she seemed too interested in Christ's work and I wasn't sure I wanted to be there. We talked very little about it. As I found out later, she just kept on praying for me, year after year.

Then came a time when I attended an overnight retreat at Camp Montgomery near Keystone Heights. After the evening's talks and sharing, we gathered in a large room for a communion service. The priest went through part of the service, stopped, and said we were to have a 45-minute silent time before we completed our service and received our bread and wine.

We were free to go outside or sit and pray, just do whatever we wanted, in silence. It was a beautiful summer night, and there was a large lake down the hill from the room. There was some kind of platform with seats built around on it, and it made perfect seating for a time of meditation. I sat down by myself, looked out over the lake, and prayed, "Lord, sometime in the past you spoke to my wife and revealed yourself to her in a way so that she has never been the same. Tonight, Lord, I would like this to be my time and my place for you to speak to me." I could picture this 45 minutes of silence as being the perfect time for my experience, whatever it might be.

I sat there and waited for Him to speak. For the last five years, all my prayers seemed never to get much over my head. If I were in a room, it seemed they would stop at the ceiling and not get any higher. I knew my Lord, but He was so far away in the Heavens I was afraid my prayers never got up there. That night, the air was deathly still, and I believed He could hear me calling as, "come, Holy Spirit, fill the hearts of your faithful." Before you knew it, I heard the big bell sounding at the top of the hill to signal the return to the service; the 45 minutes were over. I can tell you that that was undoubtedly the quietest 45 minutes of my entire life. He never spoke a word. No rushing wind and no tongues of fire, just complete silence. The one thing I knew while walking up the hill was that no one knew what I asked for and no one would ever know He didn't answer.

When I walked back into the room we were using as a chapel, there was a long line already formed to receive our bread and wine. The ones who had received were standing by their chairs all in silence. As the line got tighter, we would stop a few seconds now and then, until it started to move. Once, while I stopped, a lady standing by her chair reached out and took both of my hands in hers, looked deep in my eyes, and then the line began to move and I moved on. Her name was Emmy Cerveny, our bishop's wife. We were not close friends. I did know who she was, and I'm not sure if she knew who I was then or not. In those few seconds without a word being spoken, Christ became real in my life. He was not a thousand miles away in the heavens. He was there in the chapel with us. He was in my brothers and sisters, and He was in the hands and eyes of the sister in Christ that I just passed. So simple, so simple. Not even a still, small voice. A few more steps up, I received my communion, and soon after, we had a closing prayer. Then the priest said the quiet time is over. You see, coming up the hill, I thought He never came in the 45 minutes we had, and after the priest said the silent time was over, I realized He wasn't even late. Although He did wait until the last few minutes, what a glorious last few minutes it was! It was a long time before I could tell this story, but since that night, she has been a spiritual aid in my life. If I have learned a lesson in this, it would be that God can speak to us, to make Christ real in our lives, using His children to help him with never a word spoken. Since that night, I never look for Him above eye level anymore, and many times we have to look down as in the eyes of a child.

After this, Bishop Frank Cerveny and his wife, Emmy, became our very dear and personal friends and remain so to this day. More than just friends, they are a most important part and inspiration to my spiritual life.

I want to try to tell you a little about a talk I heard many years ago. I was representing my church at a conference in Gainesville some 50 miles away. I was new at this, but I volunteered to go, not knowing what to expect. I was a little late finding the place in downtown in a large Holiday Inn (I think), and in a conference room. I remember opening the door and finding one seat in the very back. Bishop Cerveny was already speaking to the crowd. It was packed. I cannot tell you what in particular he said that touched me so, but when I got out of that meeting I knew I had a job to do in my church. I didn't even know what it was. I knew I could no longer just go to church, hear a sermon, sing some songs, and go home until next Sunday. I told Marianne when I got home, "I've got a job to do, but I just don't know what it is yet." Of course, I wish I could tell you the words he said, but I can't. They did, however, sink in my very soul, and have been there ever since. I wish I had the ability to pass them on to you or others. God bless him for this.

After hearing many of his sermons, talks, and having some one-to-one talking, there is one statement that stands out above all the rest. "Only God can change a heart." When I take on a "project" as I call them, in trying to do some evangelism, whether to get someone to church or to bring someone to Christ, I try to remember these words. Sometimes I succeed; many times I fail. I've done some reading on Dietrich Bonhoeffer, and if this man was asked to help negotiate the end of World War II in Hitler's prison to save his life, then he must be a pretty smart man. His teaching was, if the people will not accept you, then shake the dust off your feet and move on, because time is short. In his book, The Cost of Discipleship, he turned down Hitler's offer to help Germany and was hanged in less than a month before the war was over. Why would such a brilliant man have to give up his life to Hitler when he would have been freed in less than 30 days? Why? Why? I pray that you will help pass on these words from Bishop Frank Cerveny, "Only God can change a heart."

When does Christ become real in our lives? In His time, when God knows you are ready, and not a minute sooner.

Lord, don't mind the mule, just load the wagon.

CHAPTER 18
BE PATIENT, MY FRIEND, BE PATIENT

After Christ became real, I began to realize that He speaks to us in so many different ways. In the Bible, God spoke in dreams, in visions, on mountains, in clouds, in the handwriting on the wall, through a donkey, through prophets, and just on and on.

So today He is the same God doing the same thing – getting his message to His people through His Son and through His word.

I'd like to try to tell you about a few of these times when He seems to be getting a message across.

Once some 10 or 12 years ago, as I was told I had cancer, of course it was a shock. Then, very soon after, a good friend gave me a tape to listen to called, "A Bend in the Road," by Dr. David Jeremiah, a very popular minister on the radio and TV. God spoke to me through this tape, teaching that my life was not over and that this was just a bend in my road that I would eventually get around and move on in life. Also, the doctor had told David if he lived through his cancer, he would never be the same – meaning the trees would be greener and the skies bluer. This has become so true in my life after my cure. I look at life through much different eyes than before. The winters are just as cold, the summers are just as hot, and the rain is just as wet, but somehow I see it differently through different eyes as before. I cannot tell you about your eyes and what you see. I can only witness to you about mine.

He speaks to us also through music. You know, sometimes it's a pretty song and music and sometimes it is something God wants to tell us in this music and song.

Sometimes it is in my daily reading He seems to speak. Once I read about a Christian being allowed to speak to a group of Hindus. After telling the group the Gospel story of Jesus and His salvation story, the leader of the group of Hindus got up and made a statement to them. He said, "If what this man says isn't true, it really doesn't matter. But if what this man says is true, nothing else matters." My friend, I believe I will remember this even if I get Alzheimer's. It has been one of the most profound statements I've ever read. I pray it's worth passing on.

In this little story, He didn't use words, music, or anything except a tugging at the heart. My dad was coming home from his route of grocery stores that he inspected in his work one afternoon, and was in a big hurry. This particular weekend was to be a once-in-the-year event for our church to host an annual meeting for all the area Primitive Baptist Churches to come and visit. There would be church on Saturday and Sunday with many preachers to speak. There would be a business meeting, communion, and foot washing on Sunday. Also, many church folk would come and just go home with whoever invited them to spend the night at their home. It was very ordinary for the church members to have rooms full of visitors sleeping on the floor all over the house or on quilts and blankets.

Since this was during World War II, the roads were full of men hitchhiking or thumbing their way someplace. Most couldn't afford the bus or train ticket, and many were servicemen coming home or going back to their camp. My dad decided early on that he was not going to take the chance of picking up trouble, so he didn't pick up anyone on the road. However, on this hurried trip home as he rounded a curve some 15 or 20 miles from home, an older gentleman was walking in the same direction as Dad. His head was down and he was carrying a suitcase with no hand up trying to get a ride.

Daddy said he had no idea as to why he pulled off and let him get in. He said they didn't even talk for a few minutes as they proceeded toward Palatka where we lived. After the long silence, Daddy asked him where he was going. The old fellow said he guessed he was going to the bus station and head back home. He explained that he had hopes of finding a man named Percy Moody in Palatka to take him to a church meeting, but now it was too late, so he would just go on back home. Talk about being shocked – my dad turned to say, "I'm the man you are looking for." They had never met before. He was going on word of mouth about where Daddy lived and where he went to church. Of course, it didn't take long for Dad to figure out why he pulled off the road to pick up a total stranger not even asking for a ride. So sometimes his voice of instruction is just planted in our hearts. It's up to us to recognize it.

The old fellow did come home with Dad, and he stayed the weekend, went to church, and as the old saying goes, "A good time was had by all."

Then sometimes He uses us to do His speaking. This is a very scary thought to try to comprehend. God using me? God using my voice to relate His message to another? Oh, my, we think, I'm just not worthy. Remember, He told His disciples, "You will be my witnesses in Jerusalem," (Acts 1:8).

Of course, this asks you and me if we are going to be a bystander, or a pew sitter, just a member of a congregation, or if we are going to take up our cross and be a DISCIPLE. We do have to make the choice, don't we?

I have a little story about a couple in our church years ago. The wife was coming and was being fed by hearing the Gospel preached and learning in our Sunday school. Finally, later on, the husband comes for a short time – not at all at ease with church. One day, he told me about not learning the Bible when growing up, and he felt like now he would like to learn what it said. His question was, "Will you teach me?" Of course, I did not feel qualified for the job. He didn't ask our priest, and I had no formal training. But, if he had enough confidence in me to ask, then I could not say no. Without going into detail, I will say we did not speak the same language. Our personalities were entirely different. His next question was, "Can I come tomorrow?" Of course I said, "Sure, we will get started." Another surprise, he said, "Good, I'll be there about six o'clock in the morning." It was just getting daylight when he came. We went over and sat on the beach. I did the best I could to get started, and he listened very attentively. That was our last meeting.

Soon after, they stopped coming to church, and I felt like I had really failed at what could have been some good work for Christ. All I knew was that she would like to have continued, and he didn't. It didn't seem like I could do anymore. I must say I did feel an excitement within my heart when he said, "Teach me," but it was very short lived. I did not see them any more for a number of years. Then about a year and a half ago, we passed each other in the court house when I was paying my taxes. The expression on his face was different. He was so glad to see me, but we did not get to visit as he had to run. I could tell there was reason why he hated to hurry when we shook hands in passing. I did feel better after some years of wondering if I ran him off or if I did not handle it well. Anyway, another year or so passed, when we met at a big fish fry at our church. I was working on the line to prepare the fish for the fryers as fast as I could, when he walked up to me in a crowd of several hundred fish-hungry people. I could see the different look in his eyes even better than before. He had a few minutes now, and so did I. My grandson, Colton, was right there to take up the slack when I stopped to talk.

Remember the little wind-up toys we used to play with before batteries came in? We could wind up a little duck, and his feet would pat on the floor and kind of vibrate so it would move around like he was walking. That's as near as I can come to his conversation. He wanted to tell me all about what had happened to him since we had last seen each other. He had learned so much, experienced so much, found a Bible-believing church. It was very obvious that he had found the same Jesus that Paul found on the road to Damascus. It was the same Jesus I had found at the overnight retreat on the lake. The look in his eyes was a pleasure to see after the man I had met several years earlier that was so different. The two short phrases he left me with were, "You were the mustard seed that got it all started," and as he was leaving, he hugged my neck and said he loved me. That was only a few months ago, and I hope to see him and his wife again soon. In closing this story, I'm reminded of God's word when He assures us when He says, "My word will not come back to me void," (Isaiah 55:11). Keep in mind that He didn't say how long this "come back" would be. Be patient, my friend, be patient.

Another story that might be good to follow the one about being patient took place at the Catholic high school. Yes, the one where I said I'd never work around teenagers. There was work for Christ to be done everywhere I turned – just pick one. I have no idea what brought it up, but I found a girl who claimed she did not believe there was a God. Well, Doyle, here was a real challenge. Want to try out for this one? I felt like I should take it on since she was only in the ninth grade. Well, I won't waste your time and my paper, but this project continued on all through her high school years. As she was nearing her senior year, I asked her one day to meet me at Sonny's for lunch – which she did. We sat together again, and I quoted her Scripture in John 3:16, where it tells us that all who believe will not perish but have everlasting life. Then I quoted the harsh words to her where it says, "He who does not believe is condemned already," (John 3:18).

Next, I asked her if I got up from the table where we were eating, and as I was driving away on Highway 1, suppose someone ran into me and I was squished. WHO did she know that would carry this on after I was gone. She assured me, very frankly, that there was no one. Responsibility, my friend; I felt it lying on my shoulders. No one else, and I had already been at it for almost four years. Later on, she graduated, so now I had to check on her wherever she was working. First one burger place, and then another, every few months. Of course, when I would check on her, it would be just a short visit because she was working. Then one day, the glorious words came: "Mr. Moody, I believe." After five years. Thank you, Lord – I believe. We didn't have but a minute to talk, so I asked her how it happened. I must know what led to this moment I'd worked on for so long. She just smiled and said as she was working the kitchen at a chicken place, she looked at the clock and it was 6:24, and she believed there was a God. At 6:23, she did not believe. That was all there was to it. It seems like I just don't have the right words here to say it was not the way I had planned it at all. Lord, you mean to tell me that I spent five years with this child trying as best as I could to make her a believer, and you accomplished it in the 60 seconds between 6:23 and 6:24 in the kitchen of a fast food place? Guess what? He didn't say a thing, but left me with the feeling that if He did, it would have been, "Yes, I believe you're right." It took about two more years for her to believe in God's Son Jesus. We did that in the parking lot of another restaurant in St. Augustine with her young daughter sitting beside us. At this writing, I've lost track of her again, but the story isn't over; I'll find her again to see how she is doing. Be patient, my friend, be patient.

Oh, I almost forgot to tell you, a long time after she became a believer and I found where she worked, I went by just to say hi. She came out of the kitchen door just long enough to speak, and said she had to get back to work. I said, "Can you remember when you first believed?" As she turned, she said "Oh, no, I don't remember that kind of stuff." The door closed, and then just cracked open again enough for her to say, "6:24," and then it closed for good. I then knew she and I would never forget this time.

There was another experiment that I tried when I worked with those children. They all seemed to like me and respect me and wanted to be my friend. Most of the time, they were a joy to be around. Mr. Moody was their friend. Many times I was asked to listen to problems that they didn't want to talk to the teacher or principal or guidance counselor about. I would fix their broken things and help them with class projects, and just on and on. All but one boy. He did not like me, and I still don't know why. It was in the days when long hair on boys was going out of style, and he was the only one in the school that would not get his cut. As a matter of fact, he had very pretty long, blond hair, and kept it very clean. I tried to be nice to him because I sort of hated to have all those children my friend except him. So, one day I decided that I had to get rid of this enemy, and the only way to do it was to make him my friend. Now, it did take some time on my part and some more of this patience we have been talking about, but I won and he lost. Remember now, I was the maintenance man there, and so many times there were things to load or unload, and when I needed an extra hand, I had to call on the children to help. This was when I could call on him for whatever I needed. He was my friend and I was his. He would never turn me down when I needed him.

I guess we never know when we are helping a child to mature and get through teenage years. There was one young lady that just seemed to say the wrong thing at the wrong time over and over. She had to go out of class, sit in the office, and get a note to come back to class. I can still see the frown on her face – I'm in trouble again. I could not correct the problem; all I could do was to give her a word of encouragement now and then to let her know she needed to work on her relationship with the teachers and just let her know I cared. Most of what I did I never realized I was helping her with her problems. She graduated from St. Joseph and went on to college at Jacksonville University. I'm sure by then she had made many close friends, but when graduation time came, with limited space in the university, she was allowed four tickets. Two for Mom and Dad, and two for Doyle and Marianne. Now, that in itself should have been about the highest honor I could receive, but it wasn't. After the ceremony was over and we got our hug, her dad walked up to me, shook my hand and said, "You probably helped my daughter more than all the teachers in high school." My friend, you just can't get a higher compliment than that. There are very few of these in a lifetime.

Lord, don't mind the mule, just load the wagon.

CHAPTER 19
IS THE DEVIL REAL?

You may be wondering, and you may not know for sure, or yes, you may know for sure that he is real. I pray that this chapter will strengthen the ones of you who know, and help the ones that are not sure to decide what is true.

I'm not an authority by any means on this subject, but if I could help one person to become aware of the real presence of evil in the world, then this chapter will be worth it.

With a lifetime of reading, listening to sermons, talks, witnesses, stories about miracles happening to people, I came to a conclusion. I just don't hear much about the devil and how very powerful he is. Looking back at my Christian information I've been given through the years, most of it is about God and how to meet His son Jesus. The fun part of it is talking about God and His mercy and the life we can live when we accept His son as our personal savior. Think about it for a minute in your reading and listening – of what a life we can have if we will accept the offer of Christ. We will have power, protection, never be left, His love, His understanding, and the most desired of all, eternal life.

So this belief boils down into two main categories. What will happen if you do – and what will happen if you don't. This little message is not about what will happen if you don't, I'll leave that up to you to work out. It's about this evil force, real and alive in our world today. Does it cause people around us to do things we don't understand? Yes, it does. I'm sure the people around the man in the fifth chapter of Mark who broke all the chains that bound him wondered why he would do that. They must have wondered why the force that went into the pigs caused them to jump off a cliff (Mark 5:1-13). Why would a person like Judas betray the Son of God after he had been chosen to become a special one to carry on the most important message of all time? It's because of the devil and the power that he has on this earth. Why does our

God allow this? I don't have a clue; maybe I'll just ask Him someday. In the meantime, I'm aware that he is real, and I want you to know this, too.

As we are hearing the messages of Christ and His power, we need to be aware of Satan and his power on this earth today. Did Jesus gather everyone in the towns and villages and say to them, "Come and hear what I need to tell you"? Did He put up signs on billboards saying that He would be on the Mount of Olives for a very important message that everyone should hear? Be there – don't be late. No, He just picked twelve to make sure they heard the message at very close range, and He depended upon them to tell the others as they saw fit and in whatever way they chose. Do you believe He is still doing this today? I do.

Here is another example. No matter where you live, you probably have heard of a hurricane and the wild force of its wind. You have read about them in Florida, or seen pictures or talked to someone you knew personally that witnessed one first hand. Or maybe you have been in one yourself. If you happen to be one of God's children that has had a personal encounter with the devil yourself, just skip this chapter and move on to the next. If not, read on.

Going back to the hurricanes, how do I know? Very simple – I've been there. I was the only one awake all night just wondering if we would lose the house with our family and little nieces and nephews. Praise God, it held together. You might ask if it is calm in the eye of the hurricane. Yes, I've been there. A short time before, you are afraid for your life and then you walk outside in the yard in the middle of the night in a total silence and peaceful calm. There is not a breath of air stirring. Did it cover the whole state of Florida? No, it was just a small, calm circle on the St. John's River around Palatka. But I'm here to say that the few who were there won't ever forget it and can tell you all about that night in the 1960's after the eye passed by. There is one catch: if you want to capture this information for your own, then you must trust the person enough that was there to believe it happened. What I am trying to say is, if you have ever been in the eye of a hurricane or met the devil, you won't forget either one.

Now let's go back and talk just a few more lines about the devil.

Doyle knows for sure that he is real. A personal friend had an evil spirit and came to me for help. It was just as ugly as it was in the stories in the bible, just as ugly as it is in the movies men have made about it. Yes, I have felt his power moving the muscles in a living body, twisting and turning. Yes, I have heard the voice of the evil one come out of the mouth of a personal friend. Loud and clear with no mistake of who it was. Yes, I know what it is like to stay on your knees for five hours in prayer and not move when time seems to stand still. How do I know he is real? Because I've been there, felt him, and heard his voice, and I hope I never have to hear it again. Was I glad I was there? No. But if God wanted me to be there so I would know for sure if he was real, then I will accept this as a teaching from our Savior. Did He have me there so as to help you, my reader, know for sure? Maybe so.

I am for sure that I don't want to be in another hurricane to see how calm the eye is. I've been there once, and once is enough for anybody. And I'm also sure that I never want to have an encounter with the evil one again. The only reason I wrote the chapter was so maybe you won't have to ever meet him either.

Here is another short one on the subject of the devil and how he works. My friend and principal of the high school where I worked had become such a friend that I wanted him and his wife to experience a Cursillo weekend through his church as Marianne and I had through ours years ago. Since I had had some years to see just how much the devil was against this movement, I felt like I needed to warn them. I'll say that most people attending this weekend receive a change in their spiritual lives - some more, some less, but nevertheless, a change for the better.

So first I talked to his wife in private so as not to scare him but to let her know this weekend was a very serious step in someone's Christian life. It was also to say that I knew for sure the devil did not want it to happen. It would not further his cause in any way. She listened respectfully and didn't comment much. Well, the day before he was to leave for his weekend, everything just fell apart. Everything about the job went wrong and he lost his temper and became very upset. His wife happened to come by the school. The first chance she had to catch me by myself, she asked, "What in the world is wrong with my husband?" She was seeing him behave in a way she didn't understand. It was then that I reminded her of our earlier conversation about what might happen just before he went. She just couldn't believe it, but I had seen this so many times that it didn't surprise me at all. Only I had to work a little harder to convince him that no matter what, he needed to go. Well, I'm proud to say we won, the devil lost, and they saw God's grace on the weekend and the devil's power trying to stop them from going. Resist the devil and he will flee from you. The only way he can win is for you to let him.

I'm not necessarily afraid of the devil because of the Scripture, "He that is in me is greater than he that is in the world," (I John 4:4). However, knowing that he is alive and is at work daily all around me causes me to live a more cautious life. Please take my word, friend, and be careful.

Lord, don't mind the mule, just load the wagon.

CHAPTER 20
BE CAREFUL WHAT YOU SAY

Remember the man in an earlier chapter who said, "If you think prayer will fix this, be my guest." Don't be laughing at God; He'll show you where His power is.

Here I was, back home and glad to be able to do a little more witnessing. Better yet, not be so afraid of giving it a try. Then one night, we were having a covered dish supper at church and some Christians from the area churches were there. A long-time friend and I were talking about doing God's work. I was telling him how being on the road had taken so much of the fear out of meeting and talking, even witnessing, to others. About this time, we were having our class reunion of around 35 years or so, and I was asked to offer prayer. I wasn't afraid; God was there, too. In homes or hospitals, wherever, I would pray for a brother or sister. If I was needed to listen to a problem, that would be OK, too.

I remember telling him that night that the one thing I didn't believe I could do is conduct a funeral, and thank God this was not my job and, as a layman, would never be. Some of us might be capable of doing a lot of different kinds of services in God's kingdom, but funerals, my friend, are not mine. I was proud to tell him that God didn't require me to even attempt this sort of work, and for that I was grateful. Besides, I'm much too emotional for this. My feelings would get in the way, and it would be very embarrassing to me and for the family.

Well, the bad part was, I didn't just think this in my heart, I said this out loud before my friend, and most of all, before God himself.

Without reading on ahead, you might guess what happened. In about three weeks, the phone rings, and I learn that one of my classmates is in a coma and very near death. Her family and close friends, after her death, wanted me to conduct a service for her on the front lawn of her home. They wanted me to have time to consider this and have time to prepare myself. How could I say no to her family and to my classmates and to my friend? To make the story a little clearer, she was not just a classmate, she was my close friend. She was a very popular girl, and always dated older boys in a grade or two ahead of us. She lived less than two blocks from me, so she was also my neighbor. We still had the family grocery store then, and when she bought a bag of groceries, I would drop everything and take them home for her, and then we would laugh and talk on her front porch for a while. Sometimes, at night when she wasn't dating, I would go over and she would make us a batch of chocolate fudge. Boy, was it good! We were just buddies, you know. There were many times in high school when she would miss some class because of sickness, and of course, get behind in her lessons. Always, when she came back, I would give her my notes so that she could copy and catch up. We went to a movie once, together, so that was the only real date we ever had. When we got to be seniors and looking forward to the great graduation day, she told me that I had helped her so much in school, if she made it she was going to sit by me at graduation and nowhere else. Then came the day for practice for graduation night. Our history teacher, Mrs. W.W. Carter that we had for four years, was in charge. She called the names in alphabetical order so we could line up, and my friend would get right behind me. Of course, Mrs. Carter would shout at her for being out of her place. After practice, I said, "You just can't do it; Mrs. Carter just won't let you." I think we were the first class to graduate on the football field because of outgrowing the school auditorium. She said, "When we get to the field and start marching out, it will be too late." As we were marching out the sidelines fence and onto the field, she slipped out of her place and up behind me. She whispered, "I told you I'd make it."

With this little bit of background, you can see that this phone call to prepare for a service at the death of my friend was one with much emotion involved.

After hearing the news of her condition, I went to the hospital to see her. I remember walking into her room and seeing a lady barely alive, in a deep coma. Had I not asked where she was, I'm sure I wouldn't have known her. I said a little prayer for one that seemed to be already gone, and I left. A short time later she died, and the family called for me to come and plan the service.

When I walked into the living room, they had the Bible open to "In my Father's house are many mansions," and I knew it was going to be very serious. We went through the Bible reading they wanted and they left the rest up to me. After leaving, I realized that the task ahead would be difficult because of our friendship, but a large part of our graduation class still lived in and around Palatka and were planning to be there. This would be much harder than in a church. These folks remember me as a teenager – they knew the old Doyle – and now I'm going to be reading them Scriptures. For the first order of business, I told Marianne I needed some help, some supernatural help. She said she would take care of that part while I was preparing what to say. She called about five or six of her close friends for prayer at exactly the time I would begin. Boy, was I scared! I've heard some very educated ministers say that "fear not" was in the Bible 365 times, once for every day in the year. I've never counted them, but I do know that Jesus used this a lot in his teaching. My friends, on this day, I'll admit, it wasn't working. I was full of fear. Finally the moment came and a crowd of people gathered on the lawn overlooking the river. It was a beautiful setting. Of course, my first words were from John 14:1, "In my Father's house are many mansions, if it were not so I would have told you, I am going to prepare a place for you and if I go and prepare a place for you, I will come back and take you to be with me, that you also may be where I am." After reading these words, I looked up and was completely relaxed with no fear whatsoever. After some Scripture readings, I told a few stories about school and the fun we all had and I tried to leave the family in a mood as cheerful as possible. I could have talked all afternoon with the ease of telling fun things of our friend. It was a challenge and an experience I will never forget, as a lay person. It was also, I might say, a very high honor to be chosen to say the last words for my friend.

In closing this chapter, we might say there were two lessons I learned that might be of some use to you in your life. First, when you say to another one in a family or to a friend, as it was in my case, what you can't do, and you know very well that God hears you, be very careful of this.

Gideon said, "Lord, I'm the least, surely, you don't want me." Moses was doubtful about his ability, and who did God send to kill the giant but David the shepherd boy with a sling and a rock. How unprepared can you get? You see, God just might decide to prove a point with you, too. Be careful what you say, especially out loud.

The next lesson is, if you do wind up between a rock and a hard place and need some supernatural power, don't be afraid to call. He said, "I am with you always." We need to take Him at his word. Today, as I'm sitting on my porch, I'm not in the fiery furnace, the belly of a fish, or a lion's den, praise God, so I'm at a place to encourage you, fear not. My wife and those five or six friends asked God to take away my fear, and He did, simple as that. Most of the stories in this book are about a saying I like: God helps those who CAN'T help themselves. This is another one where He showed up just in time. Without Him, I would not have been able to speak at my friend's service.

Some years later, I was asked by an old friend who came up in our church to do the same for her brother. We had known the family and him as a small child, but he wasn't connected to any church at the time of his death. I said yes, of course, and again it was an honor to be asked.

As you might know, if you are going to fix a bicycle or build a house, the second time around is always easier. I was not as nervous at this one.

Another short story I want to mention here is about the very close friend that had asked me to do the funeral for her brother. Much later, she had come down with cancer and battled it for a long time. Close to the end when I called, her daughter said, you'd better come on tonight if you want to see her. I told her it wasn't possible, but to tell her I would be there in the morning – which she did. The next morning, she had already slipped into a deep coma, and was very near death. All I could do was bend over the bed and whisper a short prayer and ask our Lord, if He was ready for her to take her on home. I told her we loved her and would see her a little later on, and I'm sure I will.

I was so sorry we could not go the night before when she still knew everyone. That seemed to be all I could do. As Marianne and I walked around the end of the bed toward the door, I looked back, and the nurse was going to her side. She breathed her last.

Her family said she was waiting for me to come. I don't have any answers, but just want to say that I am glad I said goodbye, and just "maybe" she heard me.

Lord, don't mind the mule, just load the wagon.

CHAPTER 21
WHAT IS "RICH"?

Think about it for a minute: what does being rich mean to you? Maybe you have a good idea what it means and maybe you haven't. If not, join with me for a little while on this and just maybe you might look at riches or being rich in a different light.

Most things we talk about or describe to our friends are comparisons. Even most of our statements about a particular subject are still a mass of comparisons. Let me try to explain.

You might ask, "Doyle, are you tall?" I would answer, "No, I'm about 5'5" tall." So, I'm fairly short compared to other men. If you ask my youngest grandchildren, who are four and five years old and have never thought about average height, they might have a different answer. If you ask one of them, "who is tall, you or Pa Pa," they wouldn't have any problem comparing me with themselves, and so, Pa Pa is tall in their eyes. See what I'm getting at? Am I fat? Well, I weigh about 165 pounds. Am I fat or skinny, compared to whom? Am I old or young? My mom lived with us and was 94 at the time; she didn't think I was old, but my grandchildren sure do. Is it hot or cold? Well, sometimes it gets down to 30 degrees here in the winter and you might say, no, if it got to 30 degrees below, you could say it was cold. Is your house big or small, did your car cost a lot or was it cheap, is the new bridge going to be high, is your work hard or easy? Stop and ponder with me how much of our conversation is comparison to something else. So it is, I believe, with being rich. Several days ago, I went to St. Joseph Academy, the school where I worked before I retired. Walking through the parking lot, I couldn't help noticing the rows of cars. Most of the students at this high school had a car of their own their last two years. There were some that still rode buses, of course, but looking at row after row of cars, I would say that a rough estimate would be from $8,000 to $25,000 each, which is pretty impressive transportation for a school child nowadays. Not a bicycle rack on the campus. I rode a bicycle in grammar school, but I had only two blocks to walk to high school. I was well blessed. My dad had this in mind when he bought our house in Palatka. He didn't want us to have far to walk to school.

So, back to the subject of being rich. I can tell you the very first thoughts on this as a small child, and to my knowledge, I never even shared it with anyone until just recently. Some 60 years ago, I guess, I decided that if I just had all the money anyone could ever want, and no matter how much I spent it would not matter to anyone, here is what I would do: I'd go to the grocery store and buy me a whole bunch of chickens and come home, cut off all the wings, and have Mama cook them for me. I wouldn't worry about the rest of the chickens. Remember, I was so rich I wouldn't be concerned about things like that. You know, with just two wings to the chicken and not a lot of meat on them, at that, there never seemed to be enough. There was no such thing as all the wings I wanted. Understand now, that in those days, if you wanted chicken, you bought a whole one and no one had ever heard of buying a platter of wings or drumsticks or breasts. So now, don't you know, when I reach over in the meat case and pick up a package of wings, maybe four or five pounds, how rich I feel? Of course, when I get them on the table, I feel even richer. Go ahead and dig back in your childhood – what was it then that would have made you rich?

One of the fun times was going to Grandma Davis's house for a few days in the summer. We got to put a quilt or two on the back of old Emma, the mule, and go for a ride down the woody road from her house. We got to go fishing in the pond behind the house and down the road about a mile in the branch. I don't remember catching anything over three inches, but, boy, was it fun! We had to prepare the bath time a little ahead. I remember the dog fennel and weeds were about five to six feet tall around the yard, so the boys made a narrow path from the house through the weeds, which were well over our heads, then after a sharp turn we mashed down a place big enough for our galvanized wash tub. The sharp turn was, of course, so no one could see down our path to the tub. Of course, the tub had to be filled in the morning from the pitcher pump on the back porch. The well water was very cold, so the sun would warm it up and be just right for late evening. The boys had their path and tub and the girls had theirs. It was all very private. No problems – each of us stayed in our own bath area. The well at the back porch was OK to wash in, but it was not the best drinking water. All of that and water for cooking came from another pitcher pump down a path toward the barn, I guess some 50 yards away. Of course, she had her white enamel bucket just for carrying this, and anytime any of us children were there, we would go get a bucket of good water for her. Grandma had a big soft fluffy feather mattress on her bed. Thinking back now, and with air conditioning not being heard of in those days, sinking down in that mattress in June, July, and August, it was hot. Now, as best as I can recall, no boy ever thought Grandma was poor; that's just the way life was on the farm and we were happy to get to go.

Marianne said after playing all afternoon at her granddaddy's house, her aunt would take her beside the road to a ditch full of water from rain or watering potatoes, and wash her off and get her ready to go home. Granddaddy wasn't poor, that's just the way life was out there.

Remember the new bicycle I told you about, the one I had when I was in grammar school? Then, I could put the bags of beans, peppers, cucumbers, and okra in my basket and sell it to the neighborhood. Fresh vegetables right out of my garden, to their door. Rich? I never had it so good.

We were always well blessed and had plenty of food. I never remember going hungry in hard times. When my dad had to go out of town for a week at a time, I still remember him leaving Mama three one-dollar bills just before he left. In case she ran short of food, she could send us to the store for more.

I can remember going by a friend's house one night for my dad to see this man. We got inside and it was kind of dark – I don't remember why. They may not have had electricity, but there was an oil drum converted to serve as a wood heater. It was in the winter, and a big fire was burning away. On the table was one big pot of some kind of greens for supper. The table was lined with children of all ages. We stayed only a minute, and as we started out, my daddy went back and left some money. He said something about the one pot of greens with all those children to eat. So if we are going to compare, we sure weren't poor.

Let's look at another story. I didn't have TV, video games, motor scooters, three-wheelers, four-wheelers, jet skis, for they had not come out yet. However, I had a Grandpa that liked small children and had a big imagination. He had found himself some moist, rich dirt in the edge of the river swamp on the north side of Palatka. It was on the edge of Mr. Goddard's saw mill. There he planted several hills of pumpkins. They would have moisture from the swamp and plenty of room for the vines to run in the trees. I was small, so I didn't get to go to the pumpkin patch, as he called it, very much. He would take this hoe and walk down there now and then. Another one of his favorite things to do was to go to a little grill at the foot of the Memorial Bridge on the west side for a slice of peach pie. So, one summer when my cousin Pete came to stay a week or so with me, we put in for Grandpa to take us for some pie. Let me tell you, this was a big thing, to go to a diner or a grill for a slice of pie. My grandpa strung us along forever, it seemed like. He would tell us that if we didn't see him around the house, he would be either at the pumpkin patch or gone to get some pie, and if we could catch him on the way, we could go, too. Now his secret was, if he left a large green leaf off the Turk's cap bush on the sidewalk, down at the corner, he was headed for the pumpkin patch. If he left a yellow leaf off the same bush, he would be headed for the peach pie. Now the game was on! I can still see him laying those two leaves on the sidewalk and explaining how it was going to work. Whatever it took, it would be worth it for a piece of that store-bought pie. During the day, while we were playing, we had to keep running down to the corner to see if there was a leaf on the sidewalk. Of course, you can guess the outcome: he finally left the yellow leaf and allowed himself to get caught leaving for the grill to get some pie, and we got to go along with him. These were very exciting times for a little boy who has always been rich but maybe didn't always know it.

What is rich? It seems the more I write the more I realize I was never poor. Nowadays when many children get old enough for a driver's license, Mom and Dad get them a car of their own, and a lot of times it is a brand new one. Well, my day came, too. I wanted my own car, so when I got ready to go on a date, I didn't have to wait for the family car. Used cars were not only expensive, they were in short supply. It was still too close to the end of World War II for the cars to be plentiful. The government had a ceiling price on all cars, so no one could overcharge another in these times of short supply. My neighbor had a 1941 Ford, four-door sedan with a V-8 motor. It was really a nice car. This was around 1951, as best I can remember. The ceiling price on the car was $382.00; this seemed like a lot of money, but I wanted my own ride. As I said before, I worked in my mom and dad's grocery store for $5.00 a week, but by then, I was making $7.50 a week and had saved enough to get the car. Boy, what a day! I couldn't have been any happier. Talk about being rich.

Then there was the richest blessing I ever received – to meet a tenth-grade girl named Marianne, who I loved more than life itself, and she loved me. When we planned on getting married, two years later, we needed a home, of course, like everyone else. I've told you before about the mansion on the hill that cost $4250.00 and was 24 feet square. The reason I tell you again, is that it's the same size as my living room now. As I cut across the carpet from the hall to the front porch, don't you know I still see that 24-foot square house we raised our children in for a while and I feel richer than you can imagine.

Scripture says "be content with what you have," (Hebrews 12:5). This, as I got older and started to look back, helped me learn what it means to be rich.

There were times, like fishing off the Matanzas bridge catching sheepshead, my family could about out fish anyone on the bridge. Sheepshead are very hard to catch, if you don't know how. A friend at church wanted to learn how, so I told him to meet me on the bridge after work and we would teach him. On the way over, he spent $80.00 on a new fishing rod and reel and tackle. In those days, it was a fortune. While I was trying to teach him and pulling fish up just one after another, I told him my rod and reel cost $9.15 from the pawn shop. I was happy with it and it caught fish, so that's all I needed.

Let's see now, when did I not feel rich? I guess there was a period of time after I quit the paper mill and after we lost our flower business and after we lost on the trucking business, there were times we didn't feel so rich. It seemed like diesel fuel to keep warm in the winter was our biggest expense. The wind coming off the river found every crack in our old house. Finally, we decided to buy a Franklin fireplace and heat with wood. Wood was cheap, if you cut it yourself. Trouble was, I never could afford a good chain saw to cut it with. So, I spent as much time cranking on the saw as I did cutting wood. Along about that time, lightning struck nearby and knocked out our TV. We got a used one that we could afford and we were back in business. Soon after, lightning struck again and fried that one. Well, is God trying to get our attention? I didn't know, and I still don't. I have learned that just because you're a dad or a mom, all your decisions may not be right. I've made so many bad ones. But we decided that maybe we didn't need a TV. Were we right? I don't know. It didn't seem to be fair to the children. They would go to Mama's next door to watch TV. So, for the next six years, we didn't have one. I can tell you what we did:

we spent the next several winters sitting by the fire and really getting to know each other after about 25 years of marriage. I can tell you, my friend, when it's cold and you are sitting on the couch with a quilt over your legs and a fire in the stove, you don't have to wait on the commercial to talk. Those were some of the most peaceful evenings we ever spent together. I guess it's where we built a bond we were to need for the next 12 to 15 years. Everything we tried, we seemed to lose.

Once, our family car was a 1959 Volkswagen Beetle. We loved the beach and went there a lot. I remember packing the car full with our food and fishing things. It was Marianne and I and three children and a toy for each. Anna Marie was the youngest, so we had room for everything except her beach ball. There was just no way to fit it in. Well, you might know that with those tears, we had to find a way. Just let the air out and then blow it back up when we got there. No problem – there is always a way. Then, there were second hand clothes from friends, and when the light bulb burned out in the bathroom we would get the one from the hall. If it's broken, wire it back together and use it again. We didn't keep up with the Joneses; we just lived off what we had.

I well remember going to church one Sunday morning in an old Buick we had bought for $1600.00 from my brother-in-law. We had driven it for a while, and it was getting pretty shoddy. Someone had hit Marianne, and the frame was bent so it looked funny going down the road. But it did crank and run and got us around. One particular Sunday morning, in the back of my mind I dreaded to have to drive that old car up beside some very nice cars in our church parking lot. However, when I got to Hastings and was passing through a very poor section of town, we passed a one-legged man on a bicycle! Need I say more? That old car was not so bad, after all. God speaks in strange ways, doesn't He?

Along about this time, I was elected senior warden of our church. This is one who is sort of in charge of carrying on the business of the church, and is in charge even more when there is no priest. So, in a small country church, we would experience this from time to time. Thinking back on one of these occasions when we were in-between priests, I needed some advice from our Bishop Cerveny in Jacksonville. He was a very good and understanding man. I did want to look my best after making an appointment with his staff to see him at his office. I had one belt, a black one, and the belt loop on it was broken but not completely off. That would look kind of tacky to walk into a bishop's office with a broken belt loop. You know what? After I got through with some black electrical tape on that broken belt loop, you could hardly tell it was a patch. I don't think he even knew (until he reads this story).

Times like these aren't to crush us when we are down but to make us stronger in the future and to rejoice when times are better.

Maybe, just maybe, it is so I can see and appreciate how rich I am today. Don't you see, every time we have a flat tire and it can't be fixed, I can still hear the young man at the tire store in Palatka holler out, "Mr. Moody wants a 'new' tire." The day I bought my first new tire in years was a sign of better times ahead.

I know now that had it not been for those lean years, I would not enjoy my life as much as I do now. I would not know what it means to just drive up to the station and say, "Put me a new tire on this," as I did only last week. To buy a new pair of shoes, if my old ones look shoddy. To pay a bill when it comes due. To go to a little box on the wall and set the temperature on whatever you want it to be – cool in the summer and warm in the winter.

Now I hope I can explain – all of this is nice, but not absolutely necessary to be rich. Rich is a state of mind and not how much money you have, the cars you drive, and the house you live it. I started this chapter explaining many comparisons of different things. In comparison to money standards today, we are not rich, but from what God has given us in our later years, we couldn't be richer. From a man who never expected to be able to retire, I became the man who can say, "What else could I possibly want?"

I was even allowed to have cancer and be cured of it so as to look at life differently every day. Without that experience, my life each day would lack much of its richness. I believe I have enough common sense to realize we could lose a lot of these "things" as we will call them, the comforts and fun things in life. Yet, as far as being rich is concerned, I mean the real meaning of it, I think I will always be rich.

I'll even go so far as to say that you will probably never meet or read about a richer man than me.

Just think, when I leave here, my hope is grounded in the move where the streets are paved with gold.

It says in I Corinthians 2:9, "Eye hath not seen, nor ear heard, neither have entered into the heart of man, the things which God hath prepared for them that love him."

Are you rich? If you can't answer this, start counting your blessings and see if it won't help you come up with an answer.

Lord, don't mind the mule, just load the wagon.

CHAPTER 22
FIVE LITTLE SHELLS

I've saved a few things I want to share with you. Things I've saved as we would when we walk on the beach, and out of thousands of shells, we will bend over and pick up a few - just a handful to take home. They don't match, they are not the same color, and they vary in size and shape. Most of all, when you get home and take them out of your pocket, they will remind you of your peaceful walk at the beach.

This is a very simple little tale, true of course, about Marianne's dad cutting his grass one day on his summer home in North Carolina. After he had all this tall grass cut with a sickle bar mower lying on the ground, he thought, "What a waste." He called his old friend, Roy Denny, and asked if he wanted to come over in his pickup and get the little bit of hay he had just cut. Roy said, sure, he would be glad to get it and would be there sometime later on in the afternoon. In the meantime, a shower of rain fell on the fresh-cut hay. So, Roy drives up in his truck, gets out his pitchfork and starts to load the hay, still damp from the shower. Marianne's dad came out and told Roy that he had heard you couldn't get the damp hay because it would ruin and he didn't think it would be any good.

Even though I wasn't there, I can see him now. He said, "Son, this winter when everything is covered with a heavy coat of snow, you can put a wad of this grass in the manger, and a snow ball right side of it, and that old cow will eat the grass every time." I've told the story for the past 50 years, and I haven't worn it out yet.

You see, sometimes when you have something to offer and it seems to you it's not the very best, just go ahead and offer it anyway, because in comparison to what else is being offered at the time, it may be pretty good. Sometimes, it's not what we offer but it is the best we have at the time.

God does not compare my offering or service with someone else's gift. By His mercy, He says, "Bless you, my child, for this gift of whatever, at this time." Your small armful of rained-on grass may be a bigger gift than someone else's whole bale of fine alfalfa-cured hay.

Next, I want to mention that I was probably an average teenager. Times were hard around World War II. There were chores that had to be done. I don't remember myself as John Boy Walton or any of the other ones on that famous TV show. I got out of work every time I could. Yet there was wood to get in for the heater, a kerosene tank to be filled for the cook stove, furniture to be shined with a little kerosene and old underwear. There were splinters to be chopped for the wood heater, and a big garden to be hoed, and vegetables to gather. When we got old enough, there were dishes to wash.

In my rambling mind, I remember doing all these things, but not that I volunteered for the work. Still I don't remember being disrespectful when told what needed to be done.

After I got older and had a family, my responsibility changed, and I'm sure most of your lives did as well. So one of the things I picked up and kept in my pocket like the sea shells at the beach was an old saying my grandma Davis told my mom many times. She, in turn, passed it on to me. She said, "When I was outdone, I wasn't there." So now I'm passing it on to you.

I suppose if you fit it to Scripture, it would be "whatever you do, do all in the name of Jesus," (Colossians 3:17). I can't tell you how much this little saying helped me after I grew and matured. If I was going to help out in a situation, whatever it may be, it needed to be the best I could do. I don't like to be outdone even by my friends much younger than I. When I say I'll help, then I want to do my part and carry my load. May God bless her soul for leaving me this: WHEN I WAS OUTDONE, I WASN'T THERE.

This brings on the next tidbit we might put in our pocket. Not all of our help will be the most important job in the serving we are involved in. Sometimes we will hardly be noticed in serving. Yet, our part is needed to accomplish the task we are involved in. Someone in my Sunday school told us that it may take 100 people to get someone to Christ, and you may be number 28. So don't be discouraged if you are not there when it happens and will not even get a pat on the back for it at all. To help me with this, I read about the honeybees. They are so interesting and work so well at accomplishing the one thing they do best: make honey. So now as I pour out a tablespoon full of honey on my biscuit or in my oatmeal, I can think about the one small lone bee that did his part. One bee makes about 1/12 of a teaspoon of honey in his short life of about four to six weeks. This, if we will let it, might help to keep us a little more humble. Our little bit counts, but sometimes not as much as we might think. When I look at the quart of sourwood honey we get on our trips to North Carolina, 1/12 of a teaspoon seems so small for a lifetime of hard work for one bee.

Now for our next shell in our pocket. This comes from a former governor of Florida. He has been gone for many years, but his words live on in my mind. Remember what I said a while back about words not going bad and reaching on many years after we are gone? He said, "I didn't come to stay; I came to make a difference." What an inspiration to me when I read about this man saying that! I just knew I would never forget it. We all know we can't stay. Of course, when we are young and life is fast and exciting, we think life goes on – not forever, but just on and on. Then when the hair thins, turns white, and the joints start to ache when you roll out of bed, you come face to face with the fact that life will not go on forever. Just listen to that last line: "I came to make a difference." Oh, that is such a desire in my life while I'm here. I so want to make a difference, but as I search for the words to finish this little saying, I still don't know if I do. I wish as I meet new people whether Christians or non-believers, as I leave they could say their lives were a little better because our paths had crossed. I'm afraid it's wishful thinking or dreaming. Still, it is a deep desire in my heart. I can say that because of hearing this years ago, my longing to make a difference became greater.

That's four of our shells, so let's take out the last one. This one will be narrowed down to the older generations, I'll say mostly. Some of you young folks might relate to it or even better yet, remember the story until it fits you. Anyway, after my cancer treatment some years ago, I looked at the tops of my hands and they had changed so much. They didn't look like my hands anymore. The skin was very thin, and it only took a small bump to make it bleed. Why? I still don't have a clue. I guess that's one of the side effects of the treatment. This seemed to come to me all at once. Actually, I was seeing my daddy's hands through my eyes as a small child, sitting on the edge of the bed and looking at his hands. How old and wrinkled and discolored they were compared to mine. But the lesson was in all the scars on the back of my hands that I never seemed to notice before. All of a sudden they just showed up. It was a patchwork of little white streaks all over these hands. Some of them I remember, like cutting a mountain laurel flower in North Carolina when I went with my neighbors to see the mountains for the first time. I was probably too small to be carrying a pocket knife. It was very deep and took so long to heal. Then there's one I remember when I put my hand through a barbed wire fence to open a gate on a hunting trip. Of course, most of the scars I don't remember how I got them.

Now for the lesson. These scars are a reminder to me of some pain and healing I had to experience in my younger days. None of them stopped me. They were bound up and I kept going. These scars are now only a reminder of hurts and healings in the past. When the cut is taken care of, the bleeding stops, the healing takes place, and it's time to move on. Learn from it. For the next flower we cut, turn the blade away from our other hand, and the barbed wire fence, well, just take your time and be more careful.

We all have so many hurts in our lives - some in our early childhood and some maybe last week. What I'm saying is that we don't need to let it stop us from the direction we take in life or the goal we are seeking. There are going to be sharp little knives and barbed wire fences all through life. Let them be a learning experience and not a tree across the road.

I don't know about the back of your hands. Take a good look. Or better yet, look back at the scars in your life and say, "am I still nursing these?" "Have I taken the band aid off?" "Am I still showing my old friends a piece of gauze and tape of a cut that should have been healed years ago?" If so, throw that old bandage away and look up; it's a new day.

The back of my hands are such a great reminder of God's grace and that I should move on.

Lord, don't mind the mule, just load the wagon.

CHAPTER 23
GOD CONTINUES TO SPEAK TO US

I have one last story about God speaking to us. We live on a street off A1A, and I guess it's twelve or fifteen hundred feet long with a turnaround at the end. So my neighbors on the upper end of the street never ride by. I see them only as I am going out. For a long time, as I would turn in our street, something kept tugging at me to ask the lady about church. I would see her in the yard now and then, but I did not know her at all, and didn't even know what her husband looked like. After I realized this feeling of contacting her was not going away, I said to my wife, "Marianne, why don't you ask the lady in the third house on the right as we come in about church?" Well, she didn't have to think about that very long, and she said, "God has put it on your heart, he didn't put it on mine." She said that like me, she had never met her and didn't feel the need to ask. About here, we need to mention that this lady had neighbors on both sides and across the street and lots more between. We might say, "What about all these?" I must say I did not receive an urge to talk to any of them – only at box 11. So, the ball was back in my court, and the urge was still there. I still was putting it off.

A little later, our neighborhood built a very nice dock at the end of the street into the inland waterway. It is a beautiful spot to go sit, watch the boats go by, watch the dolphins go by, see the most colorful sunsets ever, pray in the quietness, and of course, fish a little now and then. So, it came about that some of the ladies decided we needed to have a dock party to celebrate our new dock - just bring a dish and come on down Saturday. Yes, the neighbor was there, but not her husband; he was working. With a lot of small talk going on and not thinking much about it ahead of time, I saw her at the table helping her plate, with no one real close to her. Now's your chance, Doyle. I eased up to get something, too, and just asked, "Do you have a church?" I finally got it out after months and months of putting it off. There, I said it. I remember her words as if it was yesterday: "No, I don't. I'm an Episcopalian, and I can't find one in the area I'm satisfied with." After we got some food, she explained that she had been raised in a small Episcopal church where everyone knew everyone, and it was kind of like a family worshipping together. Well, this is just what we have at St. Paul's, I thought. So, I explained that I, too, was an Episcopalian, and went to a small church on the river out of Hastings. She sounded surprised and asked how far it was and about how long it took to get there. Well, my good buddy, Harry Baity, who lives right across the street, had eased up to get something by then, and he heard what she had asked. Harry is a super Christian – Baptist – and helps us on our yearly fish fry. I told her that it's about 28 miles and some of that is winding through the potato farms to find the church. So Harry, responding to her question about how long it takes to get there, comes right back with, "About two days." He laughs, of course, and I thought, "Oh, no, I didn't need that." But it was all in fun, and to my surprise, she said, "OK, I'll come this Sunday." I could have fallen off the dock. How easy was that? Moving on, I said, "What about your husband?" She did not hesitate a second. She explained that they had been married 25 years and he had never been in church on a regular basis during this time, and furthermore, they never had discussed it. Well, the next Sunday, here she was, and she loved it because it was so close to what she was raised in and just what she was looking for. After church, I said I wanted to meet her husband, and I realized he probably would be a long project to attempt. It had been so easy to get her there, and she loved the church, so all I could do was give it my best try. God had other plans. The very next Sunday morning, in she walks with her dad, and then, the following Sunday, her husband. Now, being my close friend, her husband recently explained the whole story. His wife had said, "You can come with me to church or go to our niece's dance recital next Sunday." Well, didn't he make a wise choice. God does work in strange ways, and we are proud of his choice.

I could hardly believe it. After being out of church for 25 years, he had one statement: “Now that’s the way church is supposed to be.” I wish I could say all my stories could end like this, but if they did I wouldn’t be able to buy a hat to fit my head anywhere. Wal-Mart wouldn’t even be able to help me. Getting the big head is a terrible thing; it is where pride gets its foot in the door.

Soon after, they had their 25th anniversary coming up. Of course, we had become very close friends, and she told us about getting married in the “door jamb,” as she called it at the courthouse. They wanted to renew their wedding vows in the church. Everyone helped, and Marianne made them a small wedding cake, so we had a real reception for them with all the trimmings.

After cutting the cake, she got up with tears streaming down her face. She explained how hard it was to believe the church would do this for such a new couple as them. She even came up with a line as she was giving us her thanks: “all this just for us.” This was a line Marianne and I had heard in a talk many years ago. After being out of church for many years, he was a fine man and husband. Now he knows Jesus Christ as his Lord and Savior, and he has become one of the closest Christian brothers I have. She may have dropped out for a while from what she was raised in, but she is now reaping the benefits of her church family and is enjoying her new husband. These are my neighbors, my church family, and our close friends, Fred and Skylar Harlow.

God is good, isn’t He?

Lord, don’t mind the mule, just load the wagon.

CHAPTER 24
GOALS AND BACK-BURNER QUESTIONS

This little story is someone else's story, but I do think it's worth remembering. A college professor presented his class with a thought-provoking question: "What is your goal in life?" As the story was told, it covered a lot of ground. Every one of us has different goals, and they also change from time to time. Our goals in school, young marriage, and our jobs seem to change as years go on. Well, I might add, at my age my goals don't have time to change many more times. But the professor's class had so many different goals they were seeking. After they discussed them for a while, he wrote on his blackboard. He said, "I want to go to heaven when I die and take all I can with me." I'm not going to assume you understand the part "take all I can with me," because the first time I used it, the person said you should know you can't take anything with you. So just in case you are hearing it the same way, I want to say very clearly, "I want to take all the PEOPLE I can with me." Or better yet, I want to help them know how to get there even after I'm gone. These are some more words I won't ever forget.

This really spoke to me. I want to go to heaven when I die and take all I can with me, and I might add, eventually see all my family there. If we were sitting together reading this, I might be so bold to ask, do you have a goal? Are you working toward something? Do you really know what it is? Have you told anyone about it? Do you think anyone else can tell what your goal is? If you achieve your goal, how long will it last? Just a couple of more: if you don't have a goal, why not? And when will you start to find one?

I have a question that I probably won't get the answer to. Mind you, this is just one question. After writing that down, it sounds like I know all the other answers but this one. Well, I'm not going to bother you with the other million questions I'll have.

It's always made me wonder why a person would come to Christ at a certain time in their life, and what determines that time. Some come as a child, some as teenagers, some as mature adults, some in old age. Remember the thief on the cross told Jesus, "Remember me when you come into your kingdom." This was the very last little bit of his life. He could not go to church and worship as we do today. He could not do any good works, or even help anyone. He could not even move. Nothing could he do. Why did he wait? Why do we wait? Why do we come early sometimes? I don't know. Jesus said, "I say to you, today you will be with me in paradise." I want you to know now that if you haven't been able to tell, I'm not a theologian, but I can give you my opinion on this. When He said, "I tell you the truth, (comma) today you will be with me in paradise," I believe He meant just that – TODAY. Now if He had said, "I tell you the truth today, (comma) you will be with me," it could be another million years. This is found in Luke 23:43. Again, this is my opinion. Where we put the comma determines a lot about our belief.

Now for my answer to this question of why we seek and find Christ at so many different times in our lives. It came in the middle of a swamp this past hunting season. I had an old aluminum folding chair in the swamp and was deer hunting. I guess it was our peak time for our autumn leaves to fall. They were just raining down in yellows and reds with every puff of wind. Now and then a big blow would come, and the swamp would just be full of leaves floating down. Then all would be still for a minute or two and a faint little breeze would come, and more leaves would fall. So how come those leaves didn't fall three minutes ago on the big puff? That went on all morning, and in a still small voice, He seemed to say, "When you figure out about why the leaves are falling at different times, then you can start worrying about why people have different times to come to me."

After that morning, I put that on the back burner and let Him take care of them. Oh, by the way, the next weekend it was the same with the leaves – they kept on falling at different times.

This brings us to our Christmas present from our daughter, Anna Marie. Now I must admit to you that I have been an Episcopalian for many years, but I didn't know about the Advent calendar. Advent is 40 days before Christmas and looking for the Christ to come. So, it's a calendar for you to have a different reading every day leading up to Christmas. She made these little cardboard boxes about an inch square, glued them all together in the shape of a Christmas tree, with a special message rolled up on a strip of paper in each box. Over the years she had saved these little messages from various readings. I can't tell you what day it was for, but I can tell you that it was one of the most special gifts in one phrase I've ever received. It says, "CAN YOU TELL WHAT I BELIEVE BY THE WAY I LIVE MY LIFE?" That, my friend is one of the most powerful short messages I've ever read in my adult life. I can't wait to open that box each Christmas season, not ever knowing where it is. Now, read it very carefully; it either lifts us higher than the mountain or steps on our toes. You be the judge. I pray you will pass this on.

We are all on a journey someplace, and I have the hope that I have chosen my destination. The Bible we have today contains the words that give me this hope. I can't tell you if the caveman of thousands of years ago had this hope or not. As far as I know, there is no record of them having a written hope in where they were going after their death. I also can't tell you what people will say about this ten thousand years from now. But today, in this time, in Doyle's time, all I have is the Bible and its words. It says in Romans 10:9-10 that if you confess with your mouth, "Jesus is Lord," and believe in your heart that God raised him from the dead, you will be saved. For it is with your heart that you believe and are justified, and it is with your mouth that you confess and are saved. This is about all I have to depend on. I pray that in some small way in among these pages I have helped you in choosing your destination, too. If this be the case, then to God be the glory and not to me. I pray you have chosen the same destination as me. The trip at times will be hard and even seem impossible now and then. There will be long hills to climb and at times you will seem to coast down the other side. Some roads will be rocky and some smooth, some dry and some very boggy in the mud, some wide and some narrow. Some will have pretty scenery by the roadside with flowers, and some with a barren desert with no trees in sight. There will be times when you break down and not seem to move at all.

My belief is that for most of the journey, you will be pulling a load as I have on mine.

When your wagon gets full and piled high with life's trials, tribulations, and yes, even God's tests, I am here to witness that you won't have to pull it alone. Jesus will be there to help you.

Just say, Lord, don't mind the mule, just load the wagon.

EPILOGUE

X

I started watching the effects of alcohol and tobacco at about the age of 13. Later on, I paid attention to the effects of drugs, loose living, and bad language. When I saw and read about thousands of people caught up in these - and some so close I still can't write about them - it helped me make a lifelong personal decision. I saw addictions, hurt feelings to a spouse or friends, beatings, deaths, crippled-up people, fights, prison terms, child abuse, poverty, tongue cancer, throat cancer, lung cancer, liver disease – the list goes on and on.

I decided this won't happen to me, or if it does, we won't to be able to blame it on one of these. These choices I made as a young man helped direct me to try to be the person I am today.

I've told my share of off-color stories and jokes and finally stopped that, too. I smoked a few cigars and decided 52 years ago it wasn't worth the risk. My alcohol consumption consists of communion wine whenever it is offered. I realize many, probably most, of you may not agree with me on this. That's why I saved it till last. If you have enjoyed the rest of my book and disagree with this last page, simply put your thumb on the top right corner where you will find an X, and your forefinger on the back and tear this page out. You won't hurt my feelings a bit.

My daughter, Anna Marie, gave me a small piece of paper that I carry in my wallet that reads: "right is right if nobody does it – and wrong is wrong if everybody does it."

At times this helps me make a lot of my decisions. I'm not a saint, never have been and never will be.

Your friend,

Doyle